PLAY ON SHAKESPEARE

Merchant of Venice

———

Publication of Play On Shakespeare is assisted by generous support from the Hitz Foundation. For more information, please visit www.playonshakespeare.org

———

Published by ACMRS Press
Arizona Center for Medieval and Renaissance Studies,
Arizona State University, Tempe, Arizona
www.acmrspress.com

Library of Congress Cataloging-in-Publication Data
Names: Thoron, Elise, author. | Dubiner, Julie Felise, 1969- contributor. | Shakespeare, William, 1564-1616. Merchant of Venice.
Title: The merchant of Venice / by William Shakespeare ; modern verse translation by Elise Thoron ; dramaturgy by Julie Felise Dubiner.
Description: Tempe, Arizona : ACMRS Press, 2021. | Series: Play on Shakespeare | Summary: "This clear, compelling contemporary verse translation retains the power of the original iambic pentameter while allowing readers and audiences to fully comprehend and directly experience the brutal dilemmas of the play, where prejudice and privilege reign unchallenged"-- Provided by publisher.
Identifiers: LCCN 2021017573 (print) | LCCN 2021017574 (ebook) | ISBN 9780866986809 (paperback) | ISBN 9780866986816 (ebook)
Subjects: LCSH: Shylock (Fictitious character)--Drama. | Jews--Italy--Drama. | Moneylenders--Drama. | Venice (Italy)--Drama. | GSAFD: Comedies.
Classification: LCC PR2878.M4 T48 2021 (print) | LCC PR2878.M4 (ebook) | DDC 812/.6--dc23
LC record available at https://lccn.loc.gov/2021017573
LC ebook record available at https://lccn.loc.gov/2021017574

Printed in the United States of America

We wish to acknowledge our gratitude
for the extraordinary generosity of the
Hitz Foundation

∼

Special thanks to the Play on Shakespeare staff
Lue Douthit, CEO/Creative Director
Kamilah Long, Executive Director
Taylor Bailey, Senior Producer
Summer Martin, Director of Learning Engagement
Katie Kennedy, Publications Project Manager
Amrita Ramanan, Senior Cultural Strategist and Dramaturg

∼

Originally commissioned by the
Oregon Shakespeare Festival
Bill Rauch, Artistic Director
Cynthia Rider, Executive Director

SERIES PREFACE
PLAY ON SHAKESPEARE

In 2015, the Oregon Shakespeare Festival announced a new commissioning program. It was called "Play on!: 36 playwrights translate Shakespeare." It elicited a flurry of reactions. For some people this went too far: "You can't touch the language!" For others, it didn't go far enough: "Why not new adaptations?" I figured we would be on the right path if we hit the sweet spot in the middle.

Some of the reaction was due not only to the scale of the project, but its suddenness: 36 playwrights, along with 38 dramaturgs, had been commissioned and assigned to translate 39 plays, and they were already hard at work on the assignment. It also came fully funded by the Hitz Foundation with the shocking sticker price of $3.7 million.

I think most of the negative reaction, however, had to do with the use of the word "translate." It's been difficult to define precisely. It turns out that there is no word for the kind of subtle and rigorous examination of language that we are asking for. We don't mean "word for word," which is what most people think of when they hear the word translate. We don't mean "paraphrase," either.

The project didn't begin with 39 commissions. Linguist John McWhorter's musings about translating Shakespeare is what sparked this project. First published in his 1998 book *Word on the Street* and reprinted in 2010 in *American Theatre* magazine, he notes that the "irony today is that the Russians, the French, and other people in foreign countries possess Shakespeare to a much greater extent than we do, for the simple reason that they get to enjoy Shakespeare in the language they speak."

This intrigued Dave Hitz, a long-time patron of the Oregon Shakespeare Festival, and he offered to support a project that looked at Shakespeare's plays through the lens of the English we speak today. How much has the English language changed since Shakespeare? Is it possible that there are conventions in the early modern English of Shakespeare that don't translate to us today, especially in the moment of hearing it spoken out loud as one does in the theater?

How might we "carry forward" the successful communication between actor and audience that took place 400 years ago? "Carry forward," by the way, is what we mean by "translate." It is the fourth definition of *translate* in the Oxford English Dictionary.

As director of literary development and dramaturgy at the Oregon Shakespeare Festival, I was given the daunting task of figuring out how to administer the project. I began with Kenneth Cavander, who translates ancient Greek tragedies into English. I figured that someone who does that kind of work would lend an air of seriousness to the project. I asked him how might he go about translating from the source language of early modern English into the target language of contemporary modern English?

He looked at different kinds of speech: rhetorical and poetical, soliloquies and crowd scenes, and the puns in comedies. What emerged from his tinkering became a template for the translation commission. These weren't rules exactly, but instructions that every writer was given.

First, do no harm. There is plenty of the language that doesn't need translating. And there is some that does. Every playwright had different criteria for assessing what to change.

Second, go line-by-line. No editing, no cutting, no "fixing." I want the whole play translated. We often cut the gnarly bits in

Shakespeare for performance. What might we make of those bits if we understood them in the moment of hearing them? Might we be less compelled to cut?

Third, all other variables stay the same: the time period, the story, the characters, their motivations, and their thoughts. We designed the experiment to examine the language.

Fourth, and most important, the language must follow the same kind of rigor and pressure as the original, which means honoring the meter, rhyme, rhetoric, image, metaphor, character, action, and theme. Shakespeare's astonishingly compressed language must be respected. Trickiest of all: making sure to work within the structure of the iambic pentameter.

We also didn't know which of Shakespeare's plays might benefit from this kind of investigation: the early comedies, the late tragedies, the highly poetic plays. So we asked three translators who translate plays from other languages into English to examine a Shakespeare play from each genre outlined in the *First Folio*: Kenneth took on *Timon of Athens,* a tragedy; Douglas Langworthy worked on the *Henry the Sixth* history plays, and Ranjit Bolt tried his hand at the comedy *Much Ado about Nothing.*

Kenneth's *Timon* received a production at the Alabama Shakespeare in 2014 and it was on the plane ride home that I thought about expanding the project to include 39 plays. And I wanted to do them all at once. The idea was to capture a snapshot of contemporary modern English. I couldn't oversee that many commissions, and when Ken Hitz (Dave's brother and president of the Hitz Foundation) suggested that we add a dramaturg to each play, the plan suddenly unfolded in front of me. The next day, I made a simple, but extensive, proposal to Dave on how to commission and develop 39 translations in three years. He responded immediately with "Yes."

My initial thought was to only commission translators who translate plays. But I realized that "carry forward" has other meanings. There was a playwright in the middle of the conversation 400 years ago. What would it mean to carry *that* forward?

For one thing, it would mean that we wanted to examine the texts through the lens of performance. I am interested in learning how a dramatist makes sense of the play. Basically, we asked the writers to create performable companion pieces.

I wanted to tease out what we mean by contemporary modern English, and so we created a matrix of writers who embodied many different lived experiences: age, ethnicity, gender-identity, experience with translations, geography, English as a second language, knowledge of Shakespeare, etc.

What the playwrights had in common was a deep love of language and a curiosity about the assignment. Not everyone was on board with the idea and I was eager to see how the experiment would be for them. They also pledged to finish the commission within three years.

To celebrate the completion of the translations, we produced a festival in June 2019 in partnership with The Classic Stage Company in New York to hear all 39 of them. Four hundred years ago I think we went to *hear* a play; today we often go to *see* a play. In the staged reading format of the Festival, we heard these plays as if for the first time. The blend of Shakespeare with another writer was seamless and jarring at the same time. Countless actors and audience members told us that the plays were understandable in ways they had never been before.

Now it's time to share the work. We were thrilled when Ayanna Thompson and her colleagues at the Arizona Center for Medieval and Renaissance Studies offered to publish the translations for us.

I ask that you think of these as marking a moment in time.

The editions published in this series are based on the scripts that were used in the Play on! Festival in 2019. For the purpose of the readings, there were cuts allowed and these scripts represent those reading drafts.

The original commission tasked the playwrights and dramaturg to translate the whole play. The requirement of the commission was for two drafts which is enough to put the ball in play. The real fun with these texts is when there are actors, a director, a dramaturg, and the playwright wrestling with them together in a rehearsal room.

The success of a project of this scale depends on the collaboration and contributions of many people. The playwrights and dramaturgs took the assignment seriously and earnestly and were humble and gracious throughout the development of the translations. Sally Cade Holmes and Holmes Productions, our producer since the beginning, provided a steady and calm influence.

We have worked with more than 1,200 artists in the development of these works. We have partnered with more than three dozen theaters and schools. Numerous readings and more than a dozen productions of these translations have been heard and seen in the United States as well as Canada, England, and the Czech Republic.

There is a saying in the theater that 80% of the director's job is taken care of when the production is cast well. Such was my luck when I hired Taylor Bailey, who has overseen every reading and workshop, and was the producer of the Festival in New York. Katie Kennedy has gathered all the essays, and we have been supported by the rest of the Play on Shakespeare team: Kamilah Long, Summer Martin, and Amrita Ramanan.

All of this has come to be because Bill Rauch, then artistic director of the Oregon Shakespeare Festival, said yes when Dave

Hitz pitched the idea to him in 2011. Actually he said, "Hmm, interesting," which I translated to "yes." I am dearly indebted to that 'yes.'

My gratitude to Dave, Ken, and the Hitz Foundation can never be fully expressed. Their generosity, patience, and unwavering belief in what we are doing has given us the confidence to follow the advice of Samuel Beckett: "Ever tried. Ever failed. No matter. Try again. Fail again. Fail better."

Play on!

Dr. Lue Douthit
CEO/Creative Director at Play on Shakespeare
October 2020

WHAT WAS I THINKING?

Merchant of Venice
by Elise Thoron

I am a theater maker who loves working with the poetry of multiple languages on stage (even ones I do not speak like Japanese). So I was skeptical about the Play On! endeavor because the sound of Shakespeare's words, no matter how inscrutable, is integral to my experience of his plays. Could any translation maintain the power of the original poetry while clarifying meaning to contemporary audience? Lue Douthit, director of Play On! put it in a good way: "This is an experiment, it may be a bad idea, or it may be a good one, but we'll learn a lot in the doing." And that felt true to me, so I signed on. Now, after a three year process and hearing the translation of *Merchant* resonate powerfully with actors and audiences, I see great benefits. The alteration one must do in order to make Shakespeare's verse land in a contemporary ear is actually quite small. Even in translation it can still feel like Shakespeare but with your mind comprehending at the pace words are spoken — and that's magical.

The first stage of translating for me is reading the play a few times for pure enjoyment, then mulling, daydreaming, and imagining the play in my own mind. With a Shakespearean text there was the added work of uncovering the meaning of older words by following the filaments of notes on language and history that I often do not have time to track down, thinking about the characters' levels of speech, and reading some criticism about the play — but not too much. Hearing Shakespeare's language spoken by contemporary actors, I started listening to different film versions of *Merchant* and saw whatever live theater productions came my way. As with painting a house, translation is as much in the preparation as it is in the actual laying on of paint. I wanted to be familiar with the play, know its ins and outs, have lived inside it in different ways, and for it to have lived in me for some time, before even attempting to translate a word.

In order to begin I had to get over the huge hurdle of not wanting to alter a word of Shakespeare's poetry. I was even contemplating giving up the commission, but Julie Dubiner, my dramaturg, encouraged me to give it a try. So I went to the library and took out translations of the play in other languages: Russian, French, German, and Italian, and I started to peruse them. This was extremely helpful in overcoming my resistance to altering Shakespeare's text, and it gave me some kindred spirits who were changing up Shakespeare with a clear goal of making the plays intelligible to audiences in other languages. The most useful translation, and my real companion through the process, turned out to be a 1960s French translation of *Merchant* in one of their excellent paperback editions of the classics. With that in hand to jog my mind free of the original words, I began with Antonio's first speech and the difficult scene that follows by sketching and noodling around with it for days — weeks — trying to get a feel for how little intervention is possible.

With the power and beauty of the poetry in *Merchant*, I soon decided that iambic pentameter was essential to the play; that it provided the breath and unstoppable heartbeat to keep us moving through this brutal material. Thus keeping the meter and rhyme and alternating verse with prose passages, as Shakespeare does, became a given for my translation. This was probably the biggest challenge — to keep the iamb flowing while clarifying the meaning to a contemporary ear, since Shakespeare would switch up anything and everything of sense to keep to his beat. I also realized that different characters needed different levels of intervention: Shylock the least, as his original Shakespearean speech gives him the dignity and voice of an more archaic character (he's also exceedingly well written), and at the other end of the spectrum, motor mouth Gratiano feels the most modern, so he has a lot more contemporary colloquialisms.

Then there was nothing left but to get down to the nitty gritty of the work itself. I had the folio text on the left side of the page and started filling in the blank right column, line by line, scene by scene, act by act. I did most of the translation occupying the big sofa in the living room of a family house with various people coming in and out, my reading lines aloud, their commenting, my catching snatches of conversation as they passed through, or all of us sitting around talking. So my translating was done amid the lively flow of conversation and laughter, not in silence or isolation. I've always felt translations for stage benefit from speaking them aloud and being part of an ongoing dialogue. At some point, it becomes necessary to spend time alone in order to hear the characters' individual voices and the unified "voice" of the translation, but if you've done your prep work well the more "mechanical" work of translation is never "mechanical" if it's kept boisterous with people around.

After a first pass of translating the whole play, Lue and Julie had great notes that were fun to implement. It's helpful to have sharp readers who know way more than I do about Shakespeare. Then it was thrilling to all gather and hear the translation read aloud in New York with no rehearsal but just a good group of actors and the script. The only two things I requested were a racially diverse cast and a wide range of experience with Shakespeare. We had both: from a British pro who had played many Shakespeare leads to a spoken-word poet and MC, who had never encountered the Bard. I really wanted to find out if you could just pick up this translation and read the play and see what that experience would be like for different performers. It was great, so I was encouraged to continue.

We next did a workshop and public reading at LOCAL Theater in Boulder as part of their New Plays Lab, and this time we had some rehearsal and a real audience. I was thrilled that the talk back was fierce and focused entirely on the play itself, rather than the translation. There was one audience member, though, who said he had to work much harder now that he knew what was being said rather than just zoning out to the nice-sounding poetry. This play about race and prejudice is more devastating and relevant when an audience understands in real time what the characters are saying.

Often one does not have to do that much to alter the original text for better modern comprehension other than making sure the action of the speech is intelligible at the top and letting the engine of Shakespeare's poetry roll forth unaltered. For example, Bassanio's long, intricate speech as he is about to choose among the three caskets for Portia begins: "So may the outward shows be least themselves, / The world is still deceived with ornament." The first line is hard for contemporary ears to catch, yet it is a set up for the next thirty-five lines. Clarify that one line at the top in translation: "Since outward looks show least what is inside — The world is ever fooled by appearances," and our ear is attuned to the action of the rest of Bassanio's speech, where he elaborates his thesis with countless examples from different spheres of life, and we can relax and enjoy the flow of his comparisons. Or the first line of Antonio's speech about Shylock: "I pray you think you question with the Jew …" If translated: "If you think you can reason with the Jew …" then all the poetic similes he offers after become clear. Anchoring meaning and intent in the first lines of a character's speech with clear translation allows for poetic amplification, which can remain pretty much as Shakespeare wrote it.

At the culminating Play On! Festival reading in New York there were a lot of folks who had seen the play many times before, and some high school students who hadn't, and both groups seemed to connect to the play in a powerful way. Feeling the play's relevance and heightened potential to speak to our current challenging times through the translation, I keep revising. Any process of translation ends up by putting the text through an ever finer sieve of scrutiny, word by word, joke by joke (which are particularly time consuming). So even after three readings, I am still working out tangles and trying to tease out meaning without losing the bite and beauty of the verse.

What is most interesting personally about the process of translation is the sustained and ever deepening relationship with the play over time. I now have an even deeper respect — "love" may not be the right word — for Shakespeare's *Merchant of Venice*. Despite the anti-Semitism of the historical period when the play was written, at the play's core one feels the engine of humanity, its belief in our human potential for equity and mercy in our treatment of each other, and how often we fall short, as we watch the distortion racism produces in all the characters. Like many great Shakespeare plays, for me, it is not about the single lead character or key dramatic scenes, but how the poetry and ideas resonate to the periphery, to the small "incidental" moments. In *Merchant*, after the brutal trial scene in which Shylock is stripped of his wealth and sent off to convert to Christianity, we see his daughter and her gentile lover alone in Portia's Belmont, joking, quarrelling, and listening to music, unsettled in the half-light before dawn. It is a strange scene after the high courtroom drama, almost Chekhovian in mood, in which all has shifted in the lifting of a teacup, and we hear the echo of an unearthly cry like string breaking in another world. I have never seen a production of *Merchant* that puts on stage the play's full complexity and power that I've felt working with it on the page, so I am excited to think that one day this translation could open a door to a dynamic new production of this most contemporary and brutal of plays. Brilliant, because the sum of its parts never quite add up, it is devious, shifting, irrational, slippery, and as inexplicable as the subject at its core that drives it: prejudice.

Elise Thoron
January 2021

CAST OF CHARACTERS

(in order of speaking)

ANTONIO, a prominent merchant of Venice

SALARINO, friend of Antonio and Bassanio

SALANIO, friend of Antonio and Bassanio

BASSANIO, Antonio's close friend; suitor to Portia

LORENZO, friend of Antonio and Bassanio; suitor to Jessica

GRATIANO, friend of Antonio and Bassanio; suitor to Nerissa

PORTIA, a rich heiress living in Belmont

NERISSA, Portia's gentlewoman, living with her in Belmont

SERVING MAN

SHYLOCK, a Jewish moneylender; father to Jessica

PRINCE OF MOROCCO, suitor to Portia

LANCELOT, a clown; servant of Shylock; later a servant to Bassanio; son of Old Giobbe

OLD GIOBBE, blind father of Lancelot

LEONARDO, servant to Bassanio

JESSICA, daughter of Shylock; in love with Lorenzo

PRINCE OF ARRAGON, suitor to Portia

MESSENGER

MAN

TUBAL, a Jew; friend of Shylock

SALERIO, a messenger from Venice; friend of Antonio, Bassanio and others

BALTHAZAR, servant to Portia

DUKE OF VENICE, authority who presides over the case of Shylock's bond

STEPHANO/MESSENGER, servant to Portia

Jailor, Magnificos of Venice, Court Officials, Other Followers, Attendants, Musicians

ACT 1

Enter Antonio, Salarino, and Salanio

ANTONIO

In truth I don't know why I am so sad.
It wearies me, you say it wearies you;
But how I caught it, found it, or acquired it,
What stuff it's made of, what gives it birth,
I do not know: depression makes an imbecile of me,   5
So I can hardly recognize myself.

SALARINO

Your mind is churning on the ocean,
There where your cargo ships with portly sails,
Like nobles and rich townsfolk float on high,
Parading, as it were, upon the sea,   10
Outrank the dinghies, harbor tugs, and skiffs,
That curtsy to them, bow and pay respects,
As yours fly by with canvas wings outspread.

SALANIO

Believe me, if my bus'ness were afloat,
The better part of my emotions would   15
Be at sea with my ships. I'd be plucking
Blades of grass to know how blows the wind,
Peering at maps for ports with passage deep.
And every object that might make me fear
Misfortune to my vessels, without a doubt   20
Would make me sad.

SALARINO

My breath cooling my broth,
Would blow a fever in me with the thought

1

Of how much harm big winds might do at sea.
I'd watch sand in an hour-glass run out   25
And only think of shallows and of shoals,
And see my wealthy clipper run aground,
Tipping her topsail lower than her hull,
To kiss her sandy grave; I'd go to church
And see the holy altar carved of stone,   30
My thoughts would fly straight to the dangerous rocks,
Which touching but my gentle vessel's side
Would scatter all her spices on the stream,
Enrobe the roaring waters with my silks
And in a word, one instant all worth this,   35
And now worth nothing. Could I think these thoughts,
And not have the thought that such
Ventures ruined by chance would make me sad?
Say what you will, I know Antonio's
Depressed to think about his merchandise.   40

ANTONIO

No, believe me. I thank my fortune for it,
My ventures are not trusted to one ship,
Nor to one place; nor all my capital
Tied to the fortunes of this present year:
It's not my merchandise that makes me sad.   45

SALARINO

Why then you are in love.

ANTONIO

Not I.

SALARINO

Not in love. Then let's just say you're depressed
Because you are not happy; would be as easy
For you to laugh and skip and say, "I'm happy"   50
Because you're not depressed. By two-faced Janus,

2

Nature crafts some odd balls in her time:
Those whose eyes eternally squint smiles,
And laugh like parrots hearing a bag-pipe,
And others with such vinegar faces   55
They won't show their teeth by way of smile,
Though the joke be proven to get a laugh.

Enter Bassanio, Lorenzo, and Gratiano

SALANIO

Here comes Bassanio, your most noble cohort,
Gratiano, and Lorenzo. We'll be gone,
And leave you now in better company.   60

SALARINO

I would have stayed until I made you happy,
If worthier friends had not usurped my place.

ANTONIO

Your worth is very high in my esteem.
I take it your own business summons you,
And you welcome the opportunity to depart.   65

SALARINO

Good morning, my good lords.

BASSANIO

Good gentlemen, when will we laugh? Say when?
You've grown strangers to my revels — how so?

SALARINO

We'll make our pleasure to attend on yours.

Exit Salarino and Salanio

LORENZO

My lord Bassanio, since you have found Antonio   70
We two will leave you, but at dinner time
I trust you'll let us know where we're to meet.

BASSANIO

I will not fail you.

GRATIANO

You don't look well, Signor Antonio.
You have too much respect for worldly things: 75
They lose it, who buy wealth with too much care,
Believe me you are frightfully changed.

ANTONIO

The world to me, is just a world, Gratiano,
A stage, where everyone must play a part —
And mine a sad one.   80

GRATIANO

Let me play the fool.
With jokes and laughter let old wrinkles come,
I'd rather heat my liver with red wine
Than cool my heart cold with mortifying groans.
Why should a person whose blood is warm within   85
Sit like his grandfather cut in alabaster?
Sleep when he's awake, and creep into jaundice
By being peevish? I tell you what Antonio,
I love you, and it's my love that speaks:
There are those types of men who wear their faces   90
Frothed with anguish like a stagnant pond,
And in their willful stillness stand morose
In order to appear dressed in the cloak
Of wisdom, gravity, profound conceit,
As if to say: "I am the great Oracle   95
And when I open my lips — let no dog bark."
O, my Antonio, I do know these types
Who only are reputed to be wise
For they say nothing; when I'm very sure
If they should speak, would profane those ears   100
Which, hearing them, would call their brothers fools.
I'll tell you more of this another time.

4

Just don't use your melancholy as bait
To catch this minnow of reputation:
Come, good Lorenzo, say "ciao" for now —   105
I'll end my exhortation after dinner.

LORENZO

Well, we will leave you until dinner time.
I must be one of these same dumb wise men.
For Gratiano never lets me speak.

GRATIANO

Well, keep me company for two more years,   110
And you won't know the sound of your own voice.

ANTONIO

Off you go. I'll turn a talker with your spiel.

GRATIANO

Thanks, trust me, silence is only made of gold
In salt beef tongue and a whore unsold.

Exit Gratiano and Lorenzo

ANTONIO

What do you make of that?   115

BASSANIO

Gratiano speaks an infinite deal of nothing, more than any
man in Venice. His truths are like two grains of wheat hidden
in two bushels of chaff: you'll search all day until you find
them, and when you have them, they're not worth the search.

ANTONIO

Well, tell me now, what is this lady's name,   120
To whom you swore a secret pilgrimage,
That you promised to tell me of today?

BASSANIO

It's not unknown to you Antonio
How much I have run through my whole estate,
By showing a more lavish love of life   125

Than my poor means could possibly sustain;
Nor do I now complain to be cut off
From such a noble rate, but my chief care
Is to come squarely clean of the great debts
To which my lifestyle, a bit too prodigal,   130
Has left me strapped. To you Antonio
I owe the most in money and in love,
And by your love I have permission
To unburden all my plots and purposes
How to get clear of all the debts I owe.   135

ANTONIO

My good Bassanio, please let me know,
And if it stands, as you yourself still do,
Within the eye of honor, rest assured
My purse, my person, my very last resources
All lie unlocked in your service.   140

BASSANIO

In my school days, when I lost an arrow,
I shot a second shaft in selfsame way,
The selfsame flight, observing with more care,
Where it did fall, so risking a second shaft,
I often found both. I urge this childish proof,   145
Because what follows is pure innocence.
I owe you much and like a willful youth
All that I owe is lost; but if you please
To shoot another arrow the selfsame way,
Which you did shoot the first, I do not doubt,   150
Since I will watch the aim, to either find both,
Or give the second loan full back to you,
And gratefully be your debtor for the first.

ANTONIO

You know me well, and only waste our time

6

Entangling my love with circumstance.   155
Without a doubt you wrong me more
By questioning my utmost commitment
Than if you made waste all that I have.
Then do but say to me what I should do
What in your knowledge can by me be done,   160
And I am sworn to do it — therefore speak.

BASSANIO

In Belmont is an heiress richly left,
And she is fair, and fairer than that word,
Of wondrous virtues. Sometimes from her eyes
I have received fair speechless messages.   165
Her name is Portia, and no less of value
Than Brutus' Portia, Cato's daughter.
Nor is the wide world ignorant of her worth.
For the four winds blow in from every coast
Renowned suitors, and her sunny locks   170
Hang on her temples like a golden fleece,
Which makes her Belmont like the Black Sea shore,
Where many Jasons come in quest of her.
O my Antonio, if I had the means
To hold a rival place with one of them,   175
My mind envisions such profit to me
That without question I'd be fortunate.

ANTONIO

You know that all my fortunes are at sea,
I don't have money, nor commodities
To raise the ready cash, therefore go out   180
See what my credit raises in Venice.
It will be stretched even to the uttermost
To furnish you to Belmont and fair Portia.
Go right away, inquire where money is

To hire for credit, and I'll do the same,   185
I'll have it on trust, and my good name.

They exit

Enter Portia with her gentlewoman Nerissa

PORTIA

The truth Nerissa, my little body is weary of this great world.

NERISSA

You'd be weary, sweet mistress, if your miseries were in the
same abundance as your good fortune; yet from what I see,
those who live in excess are as sick as those who starve with   190
nothing. It is no small happiness to be situated in the middle: extravagance breeds white hair, while moderation lives
longer.

PORTIA

Good dictums, and well pronounced.

NERISSA

They would be better if well followed.   195

PORTIA

If it were as easy to do as to know what's good to do, churches
would be cathedrals, and poor men's cottages princes' pal-
aces. It's a good preacher that follows his own sermons; I can
more easily teach twenty times what would be good to do
than be one of the twenty to follow my own teaching. The   200
brain may devise laws for the blood, but a hot temper over-
rides a cold decree. Youth is a mad March Hare leaping over
the traps of the cripple's good counsel. But this discourse
will not lead to my choosing a husband. Oh my, the word
"choose" — I may neither choose whom I like, nor refuse   205
whom I dislike. Thus the will of a living daughter is curbed
by the will of her dead father. Isn't it hard, Nerissa? I can neither choose one, nor refuse none.

NERISSA

Your father was very virtuous, and holy men on their deathbed have good intentions. Therefore the lottery that he has 210
devised with the three caskets of gold, silver, and lead, that
whoever chooses their meaning chooses you, will no doubt
never be chosen rightly, but only by a man you rightly love.
But what warmth is there in your affection towards any of
these princely suitors already come?   215

PORTIA

Please go down the list, as you name them I will describe
each, and you can gauge my affection accordingly.

NERISSA

First, there is the Neapolitan Prince.

PORTIA

Neeeeigh — he's a colt indeed, for he does nothing but talk
about his horse, and makes a great big deal of his own merit 220
that he is able to shoe him all by himself. I am afraid my lady
his mother got lucky with a blacksmith.

NERISSA

Then there is "The County Palatine" —

PORTIA

He does nothing but frown as if to say– "if you won't have
me, then chose another." He hears merry tales without a 225
smile. When he grows old, I fear he'll become a weeping phi-
losopher being so full of unseemly sadness in his youth. I'd
rather be married to a death's skull with a bone in its mouth
than either of these: God defend me from these two.

NERISSA

What about the French lord, Monsieur Le Boune?   230

PORTIA

God made him, so let him pass for a man. In truth I know it's
a sin to mock, but he — why he has a horse better than the

Neapolitan's, a more pronounced habit of frowning than the
Count Palantine. He is every man and no man. If a cuckoo
sings, he'll start to dance; he'd fence with his own shadow. If 235
I marry him, I marry twenty husbands. If he despises me, I
forgive him, for if he loved me madly, I would never be able
to requite his love.

NERISSA

What say you to Fauconbridge, the young Baron of England?

PORTIA

You know I say nothing to him, for he doesn't understand 240
me, nor I him. He has no Latin, French, nor Italian, and you
will come to court and swear I'm penny dreadful in English;
he is the picture of a proper man, but alas who can converse
with a dumb show? How oddly he is put together, I think
he bought his jacket in Italy, his leggings in France, his head 245
gear in Germany, and his behavior everywhere.

NERISSA

What do you think of the Scottish lord, his neighbor?

PORTIA

He has neighborly charity in him, for he took a blow to the
ear from the Englishman, and swore he would pay him back
when he could. I think the Frenchman became his security 250
and bonded by taking another blow for him.

NERISSA

How do you like the young German, the Duke of Saxony's
nephew?

PORTIA

Very vilely in the morning when he is sober, and most vilely
in the afternoon when he is drunk. When he is best he is little 255
worse than a man, and when he is worst he is little better than
a beast. And if he happened to fall to his death, I could make
do without him.

NERISSA

If he should choose to choose and choose the right casket,
and you refuse to accept him, you'd be refusing to perform 260
your father's will.

PORTIA

Therefore, fear the worst and be prepared: please set a tall
glass of Rhine wine on the wrong casket, for if the devil be
within and that temptation without, I know he will choose
the wine. I will do anything, Nerissa, before I will be married 265
to a sponge.

NERISSA

You need not fear, lady, having any of these Lords. They all
have acquainted me with their determinations, which is
indeed to return home and to trouble you no more with their
suit, unless you can be won by some other means than your 270
father's rules about the caskets.

PORTIA

If I live to be as old as Sybil, I'll die as chaste as Diana, unless
I am obtained by the manner of my father's will. I'm glad this
pack of wooers are so reasonable, for there is not one among
them but that I dote on his very absence, and I pray God 275
grant them a fair departure.

NERISSA

Do you not remember my lady, in your father's day, a Venetian scholar and soldier, who came here in the company of
the Marquis of Montferrat?

PORTIA

Yes, yes it was Bassanio, or I think that was his name. 280

NERISSA

True, madam, he of all the men that ever my foolish eyes
gazed on, was the best deserving of a fair lady.

PORTIA

I remember him well, and I remember him worthy of your praise.

Enter a Serving man

SERVING MAN

The four foreigners seek to take their leave of you, mistress, 285
and there is a forerunner come from a fifth, the prince of
Morocco, who brings word the Prince, his master, will be
here tonight.

PORTIA

If I could bid the fifth welcome with as glad a heart as I bid
the other four farewell, I'd be happy at his approach. If he 290
has the condition of a saint and the complexion of a devil,
I'd rather he should confess me than wed me. Come, Nerissa,
good servant go before; while we shut the gate on one wooer,
another knocks at the door.

Exit Portia, Nerissa, and Serving man
Enter Bassanio with Shylock

SHYLOCK

Three thousand ducats, well. 295

BASSANIO

Yes sir, for three months.

SHYLOCK

For three months, well.

BASSANIO

For the amount, as I told you,
Antonio will be bound.

SHYLOCK

Antonio shall become bound, well. 300

BASSANIO

Can you help me? Will you oblige me?
May I know your answer?

SHYLOCK

Three thousand ducats for three months,

And Antonio bound.

BASSANIO

Your answer to that.   305

SHYLOCK

Antonio is a good man.

BASSANIO

Have you heard any allegations to the contrary?

SHYLOCK

Oh, no no no, no: my meaning in saying he is a good man is
to have you understand me that he suffices as a bond, yet his
means are in supposition; he has cargo ship bound to Tripoli,   310
another to the Indies, I understand moreover on the Rialto,
he has a third in Mexico, and a fourth headed for England,
and other ventures he has squandered abroad. Ships are but
boards, sailors but men, there be land rats, and water rats,
water thieves and land thieves — I mean pirates — and then   315
there is the peril of water, wind, and rocks: the man not with-
standing is sufficient guarantee, three thousand ducats, I
think I may take his bond.

BASSANIO

Be assured you may.

SHYLOCK

I will be assured I may; and so that I may be reassured,   320

I will think on it, may I speak with Antonio?

BASSANIO

If it please you to dine with us.

SHYLOCK

Yes, to smell pork, to eat of the carcass

Into which your prophet the Nazarite conjured the devil:

I will buy with you, sell with you, talk with   325

you, walk with you, and so following: but I will
not eat with you, drink with you, nor pray with you.
What news on the Rialto, who is he comes here?

Enter Antonio

BASSANIO

It is Signor Antonio.

SHYLOCK

How like a fawning politician he looks.   330
I hate him for he is a Christian:
But more, for that in low simplicity
He lends out money gratis, and brings down
The rate of interest for us in Venice.
If I can catch him out only but once,   335
I will feed fat the ancient grudge I bear him.
He hates our sacred nation, and he rails
Even there where merchants most do congregate,
On me, my bargains, and my well-earned profit,
Which he calls usury. Cursed be my tribe   340
If I forgive him.

BASSANIO

Shylock, do you hear?

SHYLOCK

I am debating of my present store,
And by the near guess of my memory
I cannot instantly raise up the gross   345
Of full three thousand ducats: what of that?
Tubal a wealthy Hebrew of my tribe
Will furnish me: but soft, how many months
Do you desire? *[To Antonio]* Rest you fair good signor,
Your honor was the last man in our mouths.   350

ANTONIO

Shylock, even though I never lend nor borrow

14

By taking, nor by giving, interest,

In order to supply the ripe needs of my friend,

I'll break a custom: does he yet know

How much you want?   355

SHYLOCK

Ay, ay three thousand ducats.

ANTONIO

And for three months.

SHYLOCK

I had forgot, three months, you told me so.

Well then, your bond: and let me see, but hear you,

I thought you said you neither lend nor borrow   360

Upon advantage.

ANTONIO

I never charge interest.

SHYLOCK

When Jacob grazed his uncle Laban's sheep,

This Jacob from our holy Abram sprung

(As his wise mother worked on his behalf)   365

To be third to inherit, ay, he was the third.

ANTONIO

What about him, did he take interest?

SHYLOCK

No, not take interest, not direct interest,

As you would say, mark what Jacob did:

When Laban and himself had come to terms   370

That lambs born speckled, splotched, not white and pure,

Would all be Jacob's as his pay; the ewes in heat,

In end of autumn turned to all the rams,

And when the work of generation was

in action between these woolly breeders,   375

The skillful shepherd peeled these special wands,

15

And while the sheep were breeding naturally,
He put the sticks in view of lustful ewes,
Who then conceiving did in birthing time
Yield multicolored lambs, and those were Jacob's.   380
This was his way to prosper, he was blessed,
And profit a blessing, if men steal it not.

ANTONIO

This was a scheme that Jacob labored for,
A thing not in his power to make happen,
But shaped and fashioned by the hand of heav'n.   385
Is this invoked to make your interest good?
Or are your gold and silver ewes and rams?

SHYLOCK

I cannot tell, I make it breed as fast.
But note me, signor.

ANTONIO

Note this, good Bassanio,   390
The devil can site scripture for his purpose.
An evil soul producing holy witness
Is like a villain with smiling cheeks,
A shiny apple rotten at the core.
Oh what a goodly surface falsehood has.   395

SHYLOCK

Three thousand ducats is a good round sum.
Three months out of twelve, let me see the rate.

ANTONIO

Well Shylock, will we be your debtors?

SHYLOCK

Signor Antonio, many a time and oft
In the Rialto you have berated me   400
About my money and my usury,
Still have I born it with a patient shrug

(For sufferance is the badge of all our tribe.)
You call me miss-believer, cut-throat dog,
And spit upon my humble Jewish garb,   405
And all for using that which is my own.
Well then, it now appears you need my help:
Go to then, you come to me and you say,
Shylock, we would have money, you say so,
You that did spit your phlegm upon my beard,   410
And boot me as you'd spurn a foreign dog,
O'er your threshold — money is your suit.
What should I say to you? Should I not say:
Has a dog money? Is it possible
A cur could lend three thousand ducats? Or   415
Shall I bend low, and in a bondman's key
With bated breath, and whisp'ring humbleness,
Say this: "Fair sir, you spat on me on Wednesday last;
You spurned me Saturday; another time
You called me dog: and for these courtesies   420
I'll lend you this much money."

ANTONIO

I will most likely call you that again,
To spit on you again, to spurn you too.
If you would lend this money, don't lend it
As to your friend, for when did friendship take   425
The profit of a pimp from his own friend?
But lend it rather to your enemy,
Who if he breaks the bond, you may with ease
Exact the penalties.

SHYLOCK

Why look how you do storm.   430
I would be friends with you, and have your love,
Forget the shames that you have stained me with,

17

Supply your present wants, and take no cent
Of interest for my money, and you'll not hear me.
I'm offering kindness.   435

BASSANIO

This were kindness.

SHYLOCK

This kindness will I show,
Go with me to a notary, seal me there
Your single bond, and in a merry sport
If you repay me not on such a day,   440
In such a place, such sum or sums as are
Expressed in the conditions, let the forfeit
Be nominated for an equal pound
Of your fair flesh, to be cut off and taken
From what part of your body it pleases me.   445

ANTONIO

Content in faith, I'll seal to such a bond
And say there is much kindness in the Jew.

BASSANIO

You will not seal to such a bond for me,
I'd rather live within my meager means.

ANTONIO

Why fear not, man, I will not forfeit it.   450
Within two months, that's one full month before
This bond expires, I do expect return
Of thrice three times the value of this bond.

SHYLOCK

O father Abram, what these Christians are,
Whose own shrewd dealings teaches them suspect   455
The thoughts of others. Pray you tell me this,
If he should break his date, what should I gain
By the exacting of this forfeiture?

A pound of man's flesh taken from a man,
Is not so estimable, profitable neither   460
As flesh of muttons, beefs, or goats. I say
To buy his favor, I extend this friendship,
If he will take it, so: if not so long,
And for my love I pray you wrong me not.

ANTONIO

Yes, Shylock, I will seal into this bond.   465

SHYLOCK

Then meet me forthwith at the notary,
Give him direction for this merry bond,
And I will go and purse the ducats straight,
See to my house left in the fearful guard
Of a worthless servant: and presently   470
I'll be with you.

Exit Shylock

ANTONIO

Go forth, gentle Jew. This Hebrew will turn
Christian, he grows kind.

BASSANIO

I don't like fair terms and a villain's mind.

ANTONIO

Come on, in this there can be no foul play,   475
My ships come home a month before the day.

Exit Bassanio and Antonio

ACT 2

Enter Morocco, a dark Moor all in white, and three or four followers
in tow, with Portia and Nerissa and their people. Flourish, coronets.

MOROCCO

Mislike me not for my complexion,
This shadowed livery of the burnished sun,
To whom I am a neighbor and close kin.
Bring me the palest creature born in the North,
Where Phoebus' rays scarce thaw the icicles,   5
And let us make an incision to test our love,
To prove whose blood is reddest, his or mine.
I tell you Lady this dark face of mine
Has made brave men afraid (by my love I swear)
The most respected virgins of our lands   10
Have loved it too. I would not change my color,
Except to steal your thoughts my gentle Queen.

PORTIA

In terms of choice, I am not solely led
By sharp discernment of a maiden's eyes:
Besides, the lottery of my destiny   15
Bars me the right of voluntary choice.
But if my father had not wagered me,
And fenced me by his wit to yield myself
To wed the winner by the means I told you,
Yourself, (renowned Prince), then stood as fair   20
As any suitor I have yet looked upon
For my affection.

MOROCCO

Even for this I thank you,

21

Therefore I pray you lead me to the caskets
To try my fortune. By this scimitar   25
That slew great Sophy, and a Persian prince,
That won three battles with Sultan Solyman,
I would out stare the sternest eyes that look;
Out brave the bravest heart on the earth,
Pluck the young sucking cubs from the she-bear,   30
Yes, mock the lion when he roars for prey,
To win the Lady. But alas, truth is
If Hercules and Lichas roll the dice,
To determine who is the better man,
The greater roll may come, by chance, from weaker hand.   35
So Hercules is beaten by his rage,
And so may I, blind fortune leading me,
Miss that which one less worthy may attain,
And die from grieving.

PORTIA

You must take your chance,   40
And either not attempt to choose at all,
Or swear before you choose, if you choose wrong
Never to speak of marriage afterwards
To any lady, therefore be advised.

MOROCCO

Nor will I not, come, bring me to my chance.   45

PORTIA

First forward to the temple, after dinner,
You'll make your fateful choice.

MOROCCO

Good fortune then,

Cornets

To make me blessed or cursed among men.

They exit

Enter Lancelot the Clown alone

LANCELOT

Certainly, my Conscience will allow me to run from this Jew   50
my master. The Fiend is at my elbow and tempts me, saying
to me: "Job, Lancelot Job, good Lancelot," or "good Job," or
"good Lancelot Job, use your legs, up you get, run away." My
Conscience says: "No, take care, honest Lancelot, take care,
honest Job, or aforementioned "honest Lancelot Job" do not   55
run, scorn ignominious flight. Well, the most courageous
Fiend bids me to pack up: "Foo-ey" says the Fiend, "Take
flight!" says the Fiend, "For heaven's sake be brave of mind"
says the Fiend, "and run." Well, my Conscience hanging on
the neck of my heart, says very wisely to me: "My honest   60
friend Lancelot, you are an honest man's son — " or rather
an honest woman's son, for indeed my father did sometimes
smack his lips — and sometimes swell — he had that taste for
— "Well," my Conscience says: "Lancelot, budge not an inch."
"Budge," says the Fiend. "Budge not," says my Conscience.   65
"Conscience," I say, "You counsel well." "Fiend" I say, "You
counsel well." To be ruled by my Conscience, I should stay
with the Jew my master, (who God forgive me), is a kind of
devil; and to run away from the Jew, I should be ruled by the
Fiend, who, begging your pardon, is the very devil himself.   70
Certainly the Jew is the very devil incarnate, and following
my Conscience, my Conscience is a kind of hard Conscience,
to offer to counsel me to stay with the Jew; the devil gives the
more friendly counsel. I will run, Fiend, my heels are yours
to command, I will run.   75

Enter Old Giobbe with a basket

GIOBBE

Master, young man, please, which way to the Jew Master's?

LANCELOT

Oh heavens, this is my truly begotten father, who being more than legally blind, in fact highly illegally blind, knows me not. I will try confusing him with clarity.

GIOBBE

Master, young gentleman, please tell me which way to Master Jew's? 80

LANCELOT

Take a right hand turn at the next turn, but then a left hand turn at the next, and, by Job, at the very next turn, take no-hand but turn down indirection to the Jew's house.

GIOBBE

Ye gods and saints, it will be a hard route to hit. Can you tell me whether one Lancelot that lives with him, lives with him or not. 85

LANCELOT

Speak you of young Master Lancelot, (watch this, I will raise a flood of tears); talk you of young Master Lancelot?

GIOBBE

No 'master', sir, but a poor man's son, his father though I say it, is an honest, exceeding poor man, and thanks be to God alive. 90

LANCELOT

Well, let his father be whatever he will, we talk of young Master Lancelot.

GIOBBE

Your honor's friend and Lancelot. 95

LANCELOT

But I pray you ergo old man, ergo I beseech you, do you talk of young Master Lancelot?

GIOBBE

Of Lancelot, if it please your mastership.

ACT 2

LANCELOT

Ergo, Master Lancelot. Talk not of Master Lancelot, father,
for the young gentleman according to fates and destinies, 100
and such odd sayings, the Sisters Three, and such branches
of learning, is indeed deceased, or as you would say in plain
terms, gone to heaven.

GIOBBE

God and Mary forbid, the boy was the very staff of my old
age, my very prop. 105

LANCELOT

Do I look like a cudgel or a doorpost, a staff or a prop? Do
you know me father?

GIOBBE

Alas the day! I know you not young gentleman, but please tell
me, is my boy, God rest his soul, alive or dead?

LANCELOT

Do you not know me father? 110

GIOBBE

Alas sir I am legally blind, I know you not.

LANCELOT

No, indeed, even if you had your sight, you might fail to
know me: it is a wise father that knows his own child. Well,
old man, I will tell you news of your son, give me your blessing, the truth will come to light, murder cannot be hid for 115
long; a man's son may hide, but in the end truth will out.

GIOBBE

Pray you, sir, stand up, I'm sure you are not Lancelot, my boy.

LANCELOT

Please, let's have no more fooling about it, give me your blessing: I am Lancelot your boy that was, your son that is, your
child that shall be. 120

GIOBBE

I cannot believe you are my son.

LANCELOT

I don't know what to think about that, but I am Lancelot the
Jew's man, and I am sure Margery your wife is my mother.

GIOBBE

Her name indeed is Margery. I'll be damned, if you aren't my
own flesh and blood. Lord be praised, what a beard you've 125
got; you have more hair on your chin than Dobbin my cart
horse has on his tail.

LANCELOT

It would seem then that Dobbin's tail grows in reverse. I'm
sure he had more hair on his tail than I have on my face when
I last saw him. 130

GIOBBE

Lord, how you've changed, how do you and your master get
along? I have brought him a present. How do you get on?

LANCELOT

Well, well, but for my own part, I have resolved to run away,
so I won't rest until I have run some distance; my master's a
true Jew. Give him a present? Give him a noose! I am starved 135
in his service. You may count every finger I have with my
ribs. Father, I am glad you have come, give your present to
one Master Bassanio, who provides sharp new liveries. If I
can't serve him, I'll run to the far corners of God's great earth.
What rare good fortune, here he comes! Go to him Father, 140
for I'm a Jew if I serve the Jew any longer.

Enter Bassanio with a follower or two

BASSANIO

You can do so, but make it speedy so supper is ready by five
o'clock at the latest. See these letters are delivered, place the
order for the liveries to be made, and summon Gratiano to

come to my lodging soon.   145

LANCELOT

To him father.

GIOBBE

God bless your worship.

BASSANIO

Gracious, what do you want with me?

GIOBBE

Here's my son, sir, a poor boy.

LANCELOT

Not a poor boy sir, but the rich Jew's man that would sir as   150
my father will specify.

GIOBBE

He has a great infection, sir, as one would say to serve.

LANCELOT

Indeed the short and long of it is, I serve the Jew, and have a
desire as my father will specify.

GIOBBE

His master and he (with due respect to your worship) are   155
scarcely kissing cousins.

LANCELOT

To be brief, the true truth of it is, that the Jew has done me
wrong, and causes me, as my father being — I hope, an old
man will fruit-ify you.

GIOBBE

I have here a dish of doves that I would bestow upon your   160
worship, my fruit is —

LANCELOT

To be very brief, the fruit are doves — the suit is impertinent
to myself, as your worship will soon learn from this honest
old man, and though I say it, though old man, yet poor man
my father.   165

BASSANIO

One speak for both. What would you?

LANCELOT

Serve you sir.

GIOBBE

That's the very defect of the matter, sir.

BASSANIO

I know you well, you have obtained your suit.
Shylock your master spoke with me today, 170
And recommended you, if it be recommended
To leave a rich Jew's service, to become
The follower of so poor a gentleman.

LANCELOT

The old proverb is well split between my master Shylock and
you sir: you have "the grace of God," sir, and he has "enough." 175

BASSANIO

That is well said. Go father with your son,
Take leave of your old master; make your way
To where I lodge. Give him bright livery,
More gilded than his fellows, see it's done.

LANCELOT

Father, go ahead. Can't get a job, can I — eh? Don't have a 180
tongue of gold — eh? Well, if there's any man in Italy has a
finer palm to swear on the Bible with — I'll have good luck.
[*Looking at palm of his hand.*] Good grief, look, I have an ordinary life line here: a small trifle of wives, alas, fifteen wives is
nothing, eleven widows and nine maids is standard incom- 185
ing for one man. Then to escape drowning three times, and
be in fear of my life on the edge of a featherbed, these are
ordinary scrapes. Well, if Fortune's a woman, she's a good
wench in this business. Father, come, I'll take my leave of the
Jew in a twinkling. 190

Exit Lancelot

BASSANIO

I beg you, good Leonardo, think it out:

These things once purchased, put them into place,

Then come back fast. I host a feast tonight

For my esteemed acquaintance — on it now.

LEONARDO

My best efforts will be done to do all.   195

Exit Leonardo

Enter Gratiano

GRATIANO

Where's your master?

LEONARDO

Over there he walks.

GRATIANO

Signor Bassanio.

BASSANIO

Gratiano.

GRATIANO

I have a request of you.   200

BASSANIO

You have obtained it.

GRATIANO

You must not deny me, I must go with you to Belmont.

BASSANIO

Why then you must: but listen Gratiano,

You are too wild, too rude, outspoken too,

Traits that become you happily enough,   205

And do not in eyes of friends appear as faults;

But where you are not known, they'll come across

A bit indecent, so please take pains

To calm your skipping spirit with some cold

Drops of modesty, or through your wild behavior   210
I might be misconstrued in this new place,
And lose my hopes.

GRATIANO

Signor Bassanio, listen,
If I don't put on sober habits,
Talk with respect, and swear but now and then,   215
Keep prayer books in my pocket, look demurely,
Better yet, while grace is said avert my eyes
Down to my hat, and sigh and say "Amen"
With total observance of civility,
Like one well studied in sad display   220
To please his Grandma, never trust me more.

BASSANIO

Well, we will see your bearing.

GRATIANO

But I'm wild tonight, you cannot gauge me
By what we do tonight.

BASSANIO

No, that were a shame —   225
I'd request you rather to put on
Your boldest suit of mirth, for we have friends
Intending to be merry. But go for now,
I have some business.

GRATIANO

And I go with Lorenzo and the rest,   230
But we will visit you at supper time.

They exit

Enter Jessica and Lancelot the Clown

JESSICA

I am sorry you will leave my father so,
Our house is hell, and you, a merry devil,

Did rob it of some taste of tediousness;
But you'll do well. Here's a ducat for you,   235
And Lancelot, soon at supper you will see
Lorenzo, who is your new master's guest,
Give him this letter, do it secretly.
And so good-bye, I would not have my father
See me talk with you.   240

LANCELOT

Adieu! Tears exhibit what my tongue would say, most
     beautiful pagan, most sweet Jew, if a
Christian does not play false and scoop you up, I'll be much
     surprised.
But adieu, these foolish drops do somewhat drown my manly
     spirit. Adieu.

Exits

JESSICA

Good-bye, good Lancelot.
Alas, what heinous sin it is in me   245
To be ashamed to be my father's child.
Although I am a daughter to his blood,
I am not to his manner born. O Lorenzo,
If you keep your promise, I'll end this strife,
Become a Christian and your loving wife.   250

Exits

Enter Gratiano, Lorenzo, Salarino, and Salanio

LORENZO

No, we'll slink away at supper time,
Disguise ourselves at my place, and be back in an hour.

GRATIANO

We have not made good preparations.

SALARINO

We haven't even ordered torch bearers.

SALANIO

It's vile unless we pull this off in style,   255

And better, in my mind, not undertook.

LORENZO

It's only four o'clock, we have two hours

To get ready; friend Lancelot, what's the news?

Enter Lancelot with a letter

LANCELOT

If it will please you to break the seal, its significance will be

apparent.

LORENZO

I know the hand, by faith, it's a fair hand,   260

And whiter than the paper it wrote on,

Is the fair hand that wrote it.

GRATIANO

Love news I bet.

LANCELOT

May I go sir?

LORENZO

Where are you off to?   265

LANCELOT

By Mary, to bid my old master the Jew to dine with my new

master the Christian.

LORENZO

Hold up, take this, tell gentle Jessica

I will not fail her, speak it privately.

Go gentlemen, will you prepare for our masque tonight?

I just got myself a torch-bearer.   270

Exit Lancelot

SALARINO

By Mary, I'll get on it right away.

SALANIO

And so will I.

LORENZO

Meet me and Gratiano at Gratiano's place an

Hour from now.

SALARINO

It's good. We do so. 275

Exit

GRATIANO

Was not that letter from fair Jessica?

LORENZO

I have to tell you all, she has directed

How I shall take her from her father's house,

What gold and jewels she is bringing with,

The page boy suit she has in readiness. 280

If ever the Jew her father comes to heaven

It will be for his gentle daughter's sake;

And never would misfortune cross her path;

Except for this one reason as a cause:

That she is issued from a faithless Jew. 285

Come, go with me. Peruse this as you go,

Fair Jessica will be my torch-bearer.

They exit

Enter Shylock and Lancelot

SHYLOCK

Well, you shall see, your eyes shall be your judge,

The difference of old Shylock and Bassanio.

What Jessica? You will not gourmandize 290

As you have done with me — What Jessica?

And sleep, and snore, and wear out your attire.

Why Jessica I say —

LANCELOT

Why Jessica?

SHYLOCK

Who bids you call? I do not bid you call.   295

LANCELOT

Your worship took pains to tell me

I could do nothing without your bidding.

Enter Jessica

JESSICA

Call you? What is your will?

SHYLOCK

I am invited to supper Jessica,

There are my keys, but wherefore should I go?   300

I'm not bid for love, they flatter me,

But yet I'll go in hate, to feed upon

The prodigal Christian. Jessica, my girl,

Look to my house. I am right loath to go,

There's something ill brewing against my rest,   305

For I did dream of money bags last night.

LANCELOT

Please sir go, I urge you. My new young master's

Expecting your reproach.

SHYLOCK

So do I his.

LANCELOT

And they have conspired a plan. I will not say you'll see a masquerade, but if you do, then it was not for nothing my 310 nose started bleeding on Black Monday last at six o'clock in the morning, like it did that year, which was a leap year, on Ash Wednesday in the afternoon.

SHYLOCK

    What are there masks? Hear you me Jessica,
    Lock up my doors, and when you hear the drum
    And the vile squealing of the writhing fife,   315
    Don't clamber out on to the casements then,
    Nor thrust your head into the public street
    To gaze on Christian fools with varnished faces:
    But stop my house's ears, I mean my windows,
    Let not the sounds of shallow foppery enter   320
    My sober house. By Jacob's staff I swear,
    I have no mind for feasting forth tonight:
    But I will go. Go you before me servant,
    Say I will come.

LANCELOT

    I will go before sir.   325
    Mistress look out the window for all this:
    There will come a Christian by,
    Who'll be worth a Jewess' eye.

SHYLOCK

    What says that fool of Hagar's offspring? Ha.

JESSICA

    His words were, "Farewell mistress," nothing else.   330

SHYLOCK

    The fool is kind enough, but a huge feeder,
    Snail slow in profit, and he sleeps by day
    More than a wildcat; drones hive not with me.
    Therefore I part with him, and part with him
    To one, whose borrowed purse I hope he helps   335
    To waste. Well, Jessica, go in, my girl.
    Perhaps I will return immediately;
    Do as I bid you, shut doors after you:
    "Who secures their wealth endures."

This proverb in a thrifty mind matures. 340

Exit

JESSICA

Farewell, and if my fortune not be crossed,
I have a father, you a daughter lost.

Exit

Enter the Maskers, Gratiano, and Salarino

GRATIANO

This is the gable under which we stand,
Where young Lorenzo wanted us to wait.

SALARINO

His hour is almost up. 345

GRATIANO

It's strange he's missing his appointed hour,
For lovers always run before the clock.

SALARINO

Ha! Venus' pigeons fly ten times as fast
To steal love's new made bonds, than flap their wings
To meet old obligations faithfully. 350

GRATIANO

You speak the truth: who rises from a feast
With same sharp appetite as he sat down?
And where's the horse who'll retread, yet again,
His tedious hoof prints with the same hot fire
As he did pace them first? Almost everything's 355
Pursued with greater ardor than enjoyed.
How like a yearling or a favored son,
The festive yacht sets sail from native bay,
Hugged and embraced by the whorish wind:
How like a prodigal, when she returns 360
With weather-beaten hull and ragged sails,
Lean, torn, and beggared by the whorish wind?

ACT 2

Enter Lorenzo

SALARINO

Here comes Lorenzo, later more of this.

LORENZO

Sweet friends, excuse me for the long delay,

My business, not I, has made you wait;   365

But when you fancy playing "steal a wife"

I'll wait as long for you. Then let us go

Here lives my father Jew. Ho! Who's inside?

Jessica above

JESSICA

Who are you? Tell me more to be sure,

Although I swear I recognize your voice.   370

LORENZO

Lorenzo and your love.

JESSICA

Lorenzo certain, and my love indeed,

For whom do I love so much? And now who knows

But you, Lorenzo, whether I am yours?

LORENZO

Heaven and your own thoughts are witness that you are.   375

JESSICA

Here, catch this casket, it is worth your pains.

I'm glad it's night, you cannot stare at me,

For I am so ashamed of my disguise:

But love is blind and lovers cannot see

The pretty follies that they do commit,   380

For if they could, Cupid himself would blush

To see me so transformed into a boy.

LORENZO

Descend, for you must be my torch-bearer.

JESSICA

    Why must I hold a torch up to my shames?

    It's true, they in themselves are too much light.   385

    Why it's a job of illuminating, love,

    And I should be obscured.

LORENZO

    So you are sweet,

    Even in the tasty outfit of a boy. But come at once,

    The shade of night too quickly flies away,   390

    And we awaited at Bassanio's feast.

JESSICA

    I'll lock up all the doors and gilt myself

    With some more ducats, and be with you straight.

GRATIANO

    I swear she is a gentile, not a Jew

LORENZO

    I'll be damned, but I love her heartily.   395

    For she is wise, if I have eyes to judge,

    And fair she is, if my two eyes prove true,

    And true she is, as she has proved herself:

    And therefore like herself, wise, fair, and true,

    Will she be lodged in my steadfast soul.   400

              Enter Jessica

    What, are you here? On, gentlemen, away,

    Our masking mates await us now to play.

            Exit Lorenzo and Jessica

              Enter Antonio

ANTONIO

    Who's there?

GRATIANO

    Signor Antonio?

ANTONIO

    Come, come, Gratiano, where are all the rest?   405

    It's nine o'clock, our friends all wait for you.

    No masque tonight, the wind is come about,

    Bassanio will go aboard right now.

    I have sent twenty out to look for you.

GRATIANO

    I am glad of it, I desire no more delight   410

    Than to be under sail and gone tonight.

They exit

Enter Portia with Morocco, and both their trains

PORTIA

    Go, draw open the curtains and uncover

    The trio of caskets for the noble Prince:

    Now make your choice.

MOROCCO

    The first of gold a clear inscription bears: 415

    "Who chooses me, will gain what men desire."

    The second silver, does this promise carry:

    "Who chooses me, will get as much as he deserves."

    This third, dull lead, with warning just as blunt:

    "Who chooses me, must give and hazard all he has."   420

    How shall I know if I do choose the right one?

PORTIA

    Only one will contain my portrait, Prince,

    If you choose that one then I am yours for all.

MOROCCO

    Some God direct my judgement, let me see,

    I will survey the inscriptions in reverse.   425

    What says this leaden casket?

    "Who chooses me must give and hazard all he has."

    Must give, for what? For lead? Risk all for lead?

This casket threatens; men that hazard all
Do it in hopes of glorious gain and wealth,   430
A golden mind stoops not to shows of dross.
Then I won't risk or give up anything for lead.
What says the silver with chaste lunar tone?
"Who chooses me, will get as much as he deserves."
As much as he deserves; pause there Morocco,   435
And weigh your value with an even hand.
If you are rated by your reputation,
You deserve well enough, yet well enough
May not be enough to deserve the Lady:
And yet to be fearful of deserving her   440
Would be a weak disservice to yourself.
"As much as I deserve" — why that *is* the Lady.
In birth I do deserve her, and in fortune,
In grace, and in quality of breeding:
But more than these, in love I most deserve.   445
What if I stray no further, but choose here?
Let's read once more these words engraved in gold.
Who chooses me shall gain what men desire.
Why that's the Lady! All the world desires her.
From the four corners of the earth they come   450
To kiss this shrine, this mortal breathing Saint.
The inhospitable deserts and the vast wilds
Of wide Arabia are now as thoroughfares
For princes to come view fair Portia.
The watery kingdom, whose ambitious waves   455
Spit in the face of heaven, is no bar
To stop adventurers who cross the sea
As if it were a brook to see fair Portia.
One of these three contains her heavenly portrait.
Is it likely lead contains her? It were damnation   460

To think so base a thought, it is too gross
To wrap her in coarse cloth for unknown grave;
Or will I think she is entombed in silver,
Being ten times undervalued than worthy gold?
O shameful thought, to set so rich a gem   465
In metal less than gold! They have in England
A coin that bears the figure of an Angel
Stamped in gold, engraved on the surface,
But here an Angel in a golden bed
Lies all within this tomb. Bring me the key: 470
Here I do choose, and profit as I may.

PORTIA

There take it Prince, and if my form lies there
Then I am yours.

MOROCCO (*unlocks the gold casket*)

O Hell! What have we here, a skull, a death's head,
Within whose empty eye an inky scroll;   475
I'll read the writing.

All that glistens is not gold,
Often you have heard this told;
Many a man his life has sold,
Just for my outside to behold;   480
Gilded coffers do worms enfold.
If you'd been wise as much as bold,
Young in body, in judgement old,
Your answer would not be inscrolled:
Off you go, your suit is cold.   485

Cold, indeed, and labor lost,
Then farewell heat, and welcome frost.
Portia good-bye. I have too grieved a heart
To take a tedious leave, so losers part.

Exit

PORTIA

A gentle riddance. Close the curtains, go. 490
Let all of his complexion choose me so.

They exit

Enter Salarino and Salanio

SALARINO

Why man, I saw Bassanio under sail,
With him Gratiano gone along;
I'm sure Lorenzo's not aboard their ship.

SALANIO

The villian Jew with outcries raised the Duke, 495
Who went with him to search Bassanio's ship.

SALARINO

He came too late, the ship was under sail.
But there the Duke was briefed with this report:
Lorenzo and his amorous Jessica
Were seen together in a gondola. 500
Besides, Antonio, testified the fact
They were not with Bassanio on his ship.

SALANIO

I never heard a passion so confused,
So strange, outrageous, and unpredictable,
As the dog Jew did utter in the streets: 505
"My daughter! O, my ducats! O, my daughter!
Fled with a Christian, O my Christian ducats!
Justice, the law, my ducats, and my daughter;
A sealed bag, two sealed bags of ducats,
Of double ducats, stol'n from me by my daughter, 510
And jewels, two stones, two rich and precious stones,
Stol'n by my daughter: justice, find the girl,
She has the stones upon her, and the ducats."

42

SALARINO

Why all the boys in Venice follow him,

Crying, "His stones, his daughter, and his ducats." 515

SALANIO

Antonio must not default his loan,

Or he shall pay for this.

SALARINO

Indeed, more to the point,

I talked at length with Frenchmen yesterday,

Who told me, in the narrow seas that part 520

The French and English, there lies submerged

A vessel of our country rich with freight.

I thought about Antonio when he told me

And wished in silence that it were not his.

SALANIO

You're best to tell Antonio what you hear. 525

Yet do it gradually, for it may grieve him.

SALARINO

A kinder gentleman never walked the earth.

I saw Bassanio and Antonio part,

Bassanio told him he would make all speed

In his return. He answered: "Do not rush, 530

Don't botch business for my sake, Bassanio,

But stay the thorough ripening of time;

As to the Jew's bond which he has of me,

Don't let it enter in your amorous mind.

Be joyful, and focus all your thoughts 535

On courtship and such fair displays of love

As are appropriate to your purpose there."

And then and there, his eyes being big with tears,

Turning his face, he put his arm around him,

And with emotion so intensely felt, 540

He shook Bassanio's hand, and so they parted.

SALANIO

I think he loves the world only for him.
Let's you and I go and find him now
And lighten his embraced heaviness
With some delight or other.   545

SALARINO

Let's do so.

They exit

Enter Nerissa and a Servant

NERISSA

Quick, quick, please will you draw the curtain back.
The Prince of Arragon has taken his oath,
And comes immediately to make his choice.

Enter Arragon, his train, and Portia. Flourish. Cornets.

PORTIA

Behold, there stand the caskets, noble prince,   550
If you can chose the one in which I'm locked,
Straight will our wedding rites be solemnized.
But if you fail, without more words, my lord,
You must go forth and leave immediately.

ARRAGON

I am now sworn by oath to observe three things: 555
First, never to reveal to anyone
Which was the casket I chose; next, if I fail
In choice of casket, never in my life
To court another maid with intent to marry.
Lastly, if I do fail in fortune with my choice   560
Immediately to leave you and be gone.

PORTIA

Everyone must swear to these injunctions
Who comes to venture for my worthless self.

ARRAGON

    I have already done so. Fortune aid
    My heart's hope. Gold, silver, and base lead.   565
    "Who chooses me, must give and hazard all he has."
    You must look finer before I give or hazard.
    What says the golden chest? Ha! Let me see.
    "Who chooses me, will gain what many men desire":
    What many men desire, by "many" may be meant   570
    The foolish multitudes who choose for show,
    Not seeing more than the greedy eye can glean,
    Which penetrates not to the interior,
    But like a magpie, builds its domed nest
    Exposed to the weather and rude catastrophe.   575
    I will not choose what many men desire,
    Because I'll not cast my lot with common folk,
    And link my name to the barbarous multitude.
    Why then to you, oh silver treasure house!
    Tell me once more, what adage you do bear.   580
    "Who chooses me, will get as much as he deserves":
    And well said too, for who would attempt
    To cheat fortune and try to be honorable
    Without real proof of merit. Let none presume
    To wear their dignity undeserved: 585
    O would that estates, positions, and offices,
    Were not corruptly sold; and clear honor
    Purchased only by the merit of the wearer!
    How many men should bow that now stand straight?
    How many be commanded that command?   590
    How much low peasantry would now be gleaned
    From the true seed of honor? And how much honor
    Picked from the chaff and ruin of the times
    To be refurbished? Well, now to my choice.

"Who chooses me, will get as much as he deserves." 595
Assume that I deserve; give me a key for this,
And instantly unlock my fortune here. *(Unlocks the silver casket)*

PORTIA

What do you find that makes you pause so long?

ARRAGON

What's here? A portrait of a blinking idiot
Presenting me a missive. I will read it. 600
How much unlike you are to Portia!
How much unlike my hopes and my deserving!
"Who chooses me, will get as much as he deserves"!
Did I deserve no more than a fool's head?
Is that my prize? Do I deserve no better? 605

PORTIA

To offend and judge are distinct actions,
By nature opposed.

ARRAGON

What is here?

> *By fire this seven times was tried,*
> *Seven times, judgment never lied,* 610
> *Its choice has never been denied.*
> *Some kiss shadows in their pride,*
> *They with a shadow's bliss reside.*
> *Here's a fool that I have spied*
> *Covered in silver — right by my side.* 615
> *Take what wife you will to bed,*
> *I'll forever be your head:*
> *So be gone, you are sped.*

Still more fool I will appear
All the time I linger here. 620
With one fool's head I came to woo,
But now I go away with two.

Sweet adieu. I'll keep my oath

Patiently to bear my wroth.

PORTIA

And so the candle singed the moth. 625

O these well-schooled fools when they do choose,

They have the wisdom by their wits to lose.

NERISSA

The ancient saying proves it to be true:

It's up to fate if you hang and who you woo.

PORTIA

Come, close the curtain, Nerissa. 630

Enter Messenger

MESSENGER

Where is my lady?

PORTIA

Here, what do you want my lord?

MESSENGER

Madam, there is arrived at your gate,

A young Venetian, one that comes before

Proclaiming the approach of his good lord, 635

From whom he brings most genteel greetings,

What's more (besides salutations and courteous breath)

Gifts of rich value; yet I have never seen

So likely an ambassador of love.

A day in April never came so sweet 640

To show the bountiful promise of summer,

As does this harbinger come before his lord.

PORTIA

No more, please, enough. I'm half afraid

You will soon say he is some relative,

You spend such precious wit in praising him. 645

Come, come Nerissa, for I long to see

47

Swift Cupid's post that comes so tenderly.

NERISSA

Bassanio, Lord Love, if it be your will.

They exit

ACT 3

Enter Salanio and Salarino

SALANIO

Now, what news on the Rialto?

SALARINO

Why there's still a rumor at large, not contradicted, that Antonio has a richly laden ship wrecked in the English Channel: the Goodwins, I think they call the place. A very dangerous flat and fatal, where the carcasses of many tall ships lie buried. So they say, if my report, gossip, is an honest woman of her word.   5

SALANIO

I would she were as false a gossip as ever spiced the truth, or made her neighbors think she wept over the death of her third husband. But it's true without any wagging tongues, exaggeration, or crossing over the highway of plain honest talk that the good Antonio, the honest Antonio, O that I had a title good enough to keep his name company —   10

SALARINO

Come to the point.

SALANIO

Ha, the point? Is what you said: he has lost a ship.   15

SALARINO

I hope it proves to be the end of his losses.

SALANIO

I'll say a quick "Amen" to that, before the devil curses my prayer: for look, here he comes in the likeness of a Jew. How goes, Shylock, what news among the merchants?

Enter Shylock

49

SHYLOCK

You already know, none so well as you, knew of my daugh- 20
ter's flight.

SALARINO

That's true. I even knew the tailor who made the wings she
flew away on.

SALANIO

And Shylock for his own part knew his chick could fly. So 25
then it's the nature of them all to leave the dam's nest.

SHYLOCK

She is damned for it.

SALARINO

So true if the devil be her judge.

SHYLOCK

My own flesh and blood to rebel.

SALANIO

Really, you old carrion, it rebels at your age? 30

SHYLOCK

I say my daughter is my flesh and blood.

SALARINO

There is more difference between your flesh and hers than
between jet and ivory, more between your bloods than
between red and white wine. But tell us, did you hear whether
Antonio has any loss at sea or no? 35

SHYLOCK

There's another sour deal: a bankrupt, a prodigal, who now
scarcely dares show his head on the Rialto. A beggar, who
used to come so smug to the traders. Let him look to his
bond. "Usurer" he called me, let him look to his bond — he
used to lend money at Christian rates — with no interest — 40
well, let him look to his bond.

SALARINO

But if he can't pay, surely you won't take his flesh — what good is that?

SHYLOCK

To bait fishhooks. If it will feed nothing else, it will feed my revenge. He has disgraced me, and hindered me a half a mil- 45 lion, laughed at my losses, mocked my gains, scorned my nation, thwarted my bargains, cooled my friends, heated my enemies, and what's the reason? I am a Jew. Does a Jew not have eyes? Does a Jew not have hands, organs, dimensions, senses, affections, passions, fed with the same food, hurt with 50 the same weapons, subject to the same diseases, healed by the same means, warmed and cooled by the same winter and summer as a Christian is? If you prick us do we not bleed? If you tickle us do we not laugh? If you poison us do we not die? And if you wrong us shall we not revenge? If we are like 55 you in the rest, we will resemble you in that. If a Jew wrong a Christian, what is his humility, revenge? If a Christian wrong a Jew, what should his sufferance be by Christian example, why revenge? The villainy you teach me I will execute, and it shall go hard, but I will better the instructor. 60

Enter a man from Antonio

MAN

Gentlemen, my master Antonio is at his house and desires to speak with you both.

SALARINO

We've been searching up and down to find him.

Enter Tubal

SALANIO

Here comes another of the tribe — you won't find a third to equal these two, unless the devil himself turns Jew. 65

Exit Salarino and Salanio

SHYLOCK

How now Tubal, what news from Genoa? Have you found my daughter?

TUBAL

I often came to places where I did hear about her, but cannot find her.

SHYLOCK

Why there, there, there, there, a diamond gone, cost me two 70 thousand ducats in Frankfurt. The curse never fell upon our nation until now, I never felt it until now. Two thousand ducats in that diamond, and other precious, precious jewels. I would my daughter were dead at my feet, and the jewels in her ears: would she were entombed at my feet, and the duc- 75 ats inside her coffin. No news of them, why so? And I don't know how much is spent in the search. Why you loss upon loss! The thief is gone taking so much, yet it takes so much to find the thief, and no satisfaction, no revenge. No, there's no ill luck stirring but what lands on my shoulders, no sighs but 80 my own breathing, no tears but those I shed.

TUBAL

Yes, other men have ill luck too. Antonio, as I heard in Genoa?

SHYLOCK

What, what, what, ill luck, ill luck.

TUBAL

A cargo ship sank coming from Tripoli.

SHYLOCK

I thank God, I thank God! Is it true, is it true? 85

TUBAL

I spoke with some of the sailors that escaped the wreck.

SHYLOCK

I thank you good, Tubal. Good news, good news! Ha, ha, heard in Genoa.

TUBAL

> Your daughter spent in Genoa, eighty ducats, as I heard, in
> one night. 90

SHYLOCK

> You stick a dagger in me. I'll never see my gold again, eighty
> ducats at one sitting? Eighty ducats?

TUBAL

> There were several of Antonio's creditors traveling with me
> back to Venice. They swear he cannot chose but to default.

SHYLOCK

> I am very glad of it. I'll plague him. I'll torture him. I am glad 95
> of it.

TUBAL

> One of them showed me a ring that he got from your daugh-
> ter for a monkey.

SHYLOCK

> A pox on her! You torture me, Tubal. It was my turquoise.
> Leah gave it to me before we wed. I'd never have given it away 100
> for a rainforest of monkeys.

TUBAL

> But Antonio is undone for sure.

SHYLOCK

> Oh yes, that's true, that's very true. Go Tubal, see an officer,
> engage him for me two weeks before the bond is due. I will
> have the heart of Antonio if he defaults. Were he out of Ven- 105
> ice, I could do business as I will. Go Tubal, and meet me at
> our synagogue. Go good Tubal, at our synagogue, Tubal.

> > *They exit*

> > *Enter Bassanio, Portia, Gratiano, and their train*

PORTIA

> Please linger here, and pause a day or two
> Before you chance your choice, for if you're wrong

I lose your company. So why not wait? 110
There's something tells me (but it is not love)
I would not lose you, and you know yourself,
Hate would never counsel such a feeling.
In case you do not understand me well,
Because a maiden's tongue is but her thoughts, 115
I would detain you here a month or two
Before you hazard for me. I could teach you
How to choose right, but then I'd break my oath,
Which I'll never do, so you may miss me.
But if you do, you'll make me wish I'd sinned: 120
And broken bonds with my paternal pledge.
Curse your eyes that bewitch and so divide me:
One half of me is yours, the other half, yours,
My own I could say, but if mine, then yours,
And so all yours. What wicked times are these 125
Put bars between the owners and their rights?
Although I'm yours, I am not yours, until you prove me so.
Let Fortune go to hell for it, not I.
I speak too long, but just to pass the time,
To eke it out and lengthen every hour 130
Postponing your selection.

BASSANIO

Let me chose.
To live like this is on a torture rack.

PORTIA

A torture rack? Bassanio confess
What treason is comingled with your love. 135

BASSANIO

None but that ugly treason of mistrust,
Which makes me fear enjoying my new love.
There may as well be bonds of friendship

Between fire and ice, as treason with my love.

PORTIA

Yes, but I fear you speak upon the rack,   140

Where men are forced to say most anything.

BASSANIO

Promise me life and I'll confess the truth.

PORTIA

Well then, confess and live.

BASSANIO

Confess and love

That's the truth and sum of my confession.   145

Oh happy torment, when my torturer

Can teach me answers for deliverance.

Allow me to meet my fortune with the caskets.

PORTIA

Go to then! I am locked in one of them.

If you do love me, you will find me out.   150

Nerissa and the rest, please stand apart.

Let music sound while he now makes his choice.

Then if he lose, he'll sing his own swan song

To die with music. Let's build the metaphor:

My eyes will be a stream, a wat'ry deathbed   155

For the swan's last note. But what if he wins?

What music then? Then the trumpet sounds

A royal flourish, as true subjects bow

To a monarch newly crowned. Just like those

Sweet and dulcet sounds at break of day,   160

That creep into the dreaming bridegroom's ear

And summon him to marriage. Now he goes

With no less majesty, but much more love,

Than did young Hercules, when he redeemed

The virgin tribute paid by howling Troy   165

To the Sea-Monster. I'll be the sacrificial virgin.
The rest — you over there — the Trojan wives,
With teary faces come forth to view
The outcome of the battle. Go Hercules!
If you live, so do I. I watch the fight with more dismay   170
Than you who fight and make the awful fray.

Music. A song while Bassanio comments on the caskets.

SONG

Tell me where true love is *bred*
In the heart, or in the *head* —
How begot, how nouri*shed* — reply, reply!
Is it engend*'red* in the eye,   175
With gazing *fed*, but then love dies
Right in the cradle where it lies:
Let us all ring love's death knell —
The tintinnabulation —
Of the Ding Dong bell.   180

ALL

Of the bell, bell, bell, bell, bell, bell, bell! *(To the rhythm of Edgar
Allan Poe's poem 'The Bells')*

[INTERMISSION]

BASSANIO

Since outward looks least show what is inside —
The world is ever fooled by appearances.
In court, what case so tainted and corrupt,
If but argued with a gracious voice,   185
Obscures the show of guilt? In religion,
What fault so wrong, but some sober brow
Will bless it and approve it with scripture,
Hiding vulgarity with fair ornament?
No vice so vile, but it cannot assume   190

The imprint of virtue on its exterior.
How many cowards, whose hearts are all as false
As stairs of sand, still wear upon their chins
The beards of Hercules or frowning Mars?
Search within, you'll find their liver white as milk;   195
They only take on valor's exterior form
To render them revered. Look at beauty,
And you will see it's purchased by the pound,
And make up works a miracle on nature,
Making them most wanton that wear it most.   200
And take those curly, snaky golden locks,
That make lascivious dances in the wind,
Upon examination, are oft revealed
To be the inheritance of another's head,
The skull that bred them buried in a tomb.   205
So ornament is but a gilded shore
To a most dangerous sea; a beauteous scarf
Veiling an Indian beauty; in a word,
The seeming truth, in which our time is dressed
To entrap the wisest. Therefore, you gaudy gold,   210
Hard food for Midas, I'll have none of you;
Nor you, pale silver, common currency
Between man and man; but you, you meager lead,
Who threatens rather than promises anything,
Your dullness moves me more than eloquence,   215
So you I chose, joy be the consequence.

PORTIA

How all other passions melt in air,
All doubtful thoughts and rash embraced despair,
All shud'ring fears and green-eyed jealousy.
O love be moderate, calm this ecstasy,   220
In good measure, rain your joy, stop this excess —

Too much I feel your blessing — make it less,
For I fear surfeit.

BASSANIO *(opens lead casket)*

What do I find?
Fair Portia's counterfeit. What god-like painter   225
Comes so near creation? Do these eyes move?
Or riding on my eyeballs move themselves?
Here lips are severed, parted with sugar breath,
A sigh too sweet to split up two sweet friends. Here in her hairs
The painter plays the spider, weaves a web: 230
A golden mesh to entrap the hearts of men
Faster than gnats in cobwebs. But her eyes —
How could he see to paint them? Having made one,
I think it would have the power to steal both his own
And leave the other eye undone. Yet look how far   235
The substance of my praise wrongs this shadow.
Underpraising it the same extent this shadow
Limps behind the real substance. Here's a scroll
Which contains the summary my fortune.

You who do not choose by view,   240
Have better luck and choose as true.
Since this fortune falls to you,
Be content and seek not new.
If you be well pleased with this,
And hold your fortune as your bliss,   245
Please turn to where your lady is
And claim her with a loving kiss.

A gentle scroll: fair lady, by your leave,
My orders bid me give, and then receive.
Like one of two contenders for a prize   250
Who thinks he has done well in people's eyes,
Hearing applause and universal shout,

58

Giddy in spirit, but gazing out in doubt
Whether those peals of praise be his or no.
So thrice fair lady, I stand before you so,   255
In doubt of whether what I see is true,
Until confirmed, signed, ratified by you.
PORTIA
You see me, lord Bassanio, where I am,
Such as I am. Though for myself alone
I'd not be ambitious in my wish   260
To wish myself much better, yet for you,
I'd be tripled, twenty times myself,
A thousand times more fair, ten thousand times
More rich, to be of value in your esteem,
I might in virtues, beauties, living, friends,   265
Exceed your accounts, but the full sum of me
Is the sum of nothing; to make account:
I'm an unlessoned girl, unschooled, unpracticed,
Happy in this: that she is not yet so old
But she may learn; and happier still   270
She's not bred so dull she cannot learn.
Happiest of all is that her gentle spirit
Commits itself to yours to be directed,
As to her lord, her governor and her king
Myself, and all that's mine, to you and yours   275
Be everything. Just now I was the lord
Of this fair mansion, master of my servants,
Queen of my own self; and even now, right now,
This house, these servants, and this same self
Are yours, my lord, I give them with this ring,   280
Which when you part from, lose, or give away,
Let it signal the ruin of your love,
And give me the right to condemn you.

BASSANIO

    Madam, you have robbed me of all words,

    Only my blood speaks to you in my veins.   285

    And there is such confusion in my powers,

    Like after some oration nobly spoke

    By a beloved prince, a roar arises

    Among the pleased multitude, a buzzing,

    Where every something uttered blends together,   290

    Turns into a wild of nothing, except joy,

    Expressed and not expressed. But when this ring

    Parts from this finger, then I part from my life.

    O then be bold to say Bassanio's dead.

NERISSA

    My lord and lady, now it is our time,   295

    Who have stood by and watched our wishes prosper,

    To cry: "All joy! All joy! My lord and lady."

GRATIANO

    My lord Bassanio and my gentle lady,

    I wish you all the joy that one can wish:

    For I'm sure your wishes are akin to mine.   300

    So when your honors stamp a seal upon

    The bargain of your faith, I'm asking you

    If when you wed, I may be married too.

BASSANIO

    With all my heart, if you can find a wife.   305

GRATIANO

    Thanks to your lordship, I have got me one.

    My eyes, my lord can look as quick as yours:

    You saw the mistress, I checked out the maid:

    You loved, I loved during the pit stop,

    So what pertains to me, my lord, was just like you: 310

    Your fortune rested on three caskets here,

And mine did too, as it turned out to be.
For wooing here I sweat a lot of sweat,
And swearing true — until my mouth ran dry —
With oaths of love — at last — if a promise last —   315
I got a promise out of this fair one here —
To have her love, provided that your fortune
Attained her mistress.

PORTIA

Is this true Nerissa?   320

NERISSA

Madam, it is so, if you are pleased with it.

BASSANIO

And are you Gratiano in good faith?

GRATIANO

Good faith, my lord.

BASSANIO

Our feast will be much honored by your marriage.

GRATIANO

Let's place a bet—a thousand ducats—who has the first boy—   325

NERISSA

What, the stake up front?

GRATIANO

Yes, with my stake up front, we'll win the bet.
But who comes here? Lorenzo and his infidel?
What, and my old Venetian friend Salerio?

Enter Lorenzo, Jessica, and Salerio

BASSANIO

Lorenzo and Salerio, welcome!   330
If the youth of my new position here
Has pow'r to welcome you. If you permit,
Sweet Portia, these are my friends and countrymen,
I welcome.

61

PORTIA

So do I my lord, they are most welcome.   335

LORENZO

I thank your honor, for my part, my lord,

It was not my intent to see you here.

But meeting with Salerio today,

He so implored me to accompany him,

It was beyond my ability to say no.   340

SALERIO

I did my lord,

And I have reason for it. Signor Antonio

Sends you his greetings.

Hands him a letter

BASSANIO

Before I open his letter

Please tell me how my good friend is.   345

SALERIO

Not sick my lord, unless it be in his mind,

Nor well, unless his mind wills it; his letter

Will show you his condition.

Opens the letter

GRATIANO

Nerissa, cheer up that stranger and bid her welcome.

Your hand Salerio, what's the news from Venice?   350

How fairs our royal merchant good Antonio?

I know he will be glad of our success:

We are two Jasons with the golden fleece.

SALERIO

I wish you'd won the fleece Antonio lost.

PORTIA

There are some harmful contents in that letter,   355

Which steal the color from Bassanio's cheek.

Some dear friend dead, or nothing in the world
Could so greatly alter the constitution
Of any stable man. What, worse and worse?
Bassanio, I must know. I am half yourself,   360
So I must freely share a half of anything
That this same letter brings you.

BASSANIO

O sweet Portia,
Here are a few of the most unpleasant words
Ever blotted into paper. Gentle lady,   365
When I first confessed my love to you,
I freely told you all the wealth I had
Ran in my veins — I was a gentleman —
And then I told you true. And yet dear lady,
Rating myself at nothing, you shall see   370
How big a braggart and liar I was, when I told you
My worth was nothing. I should have told you
That it was worse than nothing: for indeed
I have indebted myself to a dear friend,
Indebted my friend to his worst enemy,   375
To feed my needs. Here is a letter lady,
The paper is the body of my friend,
And every word in it a gaping wound
Spurting forth his life blood. But is it true Salerio,
Have all his ventures failed? Not one come home,   380
From Tripoli, from Mexico or England,
From Lisbon, Barbary, or India,
Not one vessel escaped the dreadful touch
Of merchant marring rocks?

SALERIO

Not one my Lord.   385
Besides, it would appear that if he had

The money present to discharge his debt,
The Jew would not take it. Never have I known
A creature that appears in shape of man
So keen and greedy to destroy a man.   390
He'll press the Duke at morning and at night,
And will impugn the freedom of the State
If they deny him justice. Twenty merchants,
The Duke himself, and all Magnificos
Of greatest import have all argued with him,   395
But none can drive him from his spiteful suit,
Of punishment, of justice, and his bond.

JESSICA

When I was with him, I once heard him swear
To Tubal and to Chus, his countrymen,
That he would rather have Antonio's flesh   400
Than twenty times the value of the sum
That was owed to him. And I know my lord,
If law, authority, and pow'r don't deny him,
It will go hard with poor Antonio.

PORTIA

Is it your dear friend that is in trouble?   405

BASSANIO

The dearest friend to me, the kindest man,
Most even-tempered, and a tireless soul
In doing good for others; one in whom
The ancient Roman honor shines more bright
Than anyone alive in Italy.   410

PORTIA

How much does he owe the Jew?

BASSANIO

For me, three thousand ducats.

PORTIA

What, no more?
Pay him six thousand and deface the bond,
Double six thousand and triple that, 415
Before the friend you have so well described
Will lose a hair through Bassanio's fault.
First, come with me to church and let us marry,
And then away to Venice to your friend.
For you shall never lie by Portia's side 420
With an unquiet soul. You will have gold
To pay the petty debt twenty times over.
When it is paid, bring your true friend back home.
My maid Nerissa and myself meantime
Will live as maids and widows. Come away, 425
For you shall leave upon your wedding day.
Bid your friends welcome, show merry cheer,
Since you are dearly bought, I'll love you dear.
But let me hear the letter of your friend.

ANTONIO

Sweet Bassanio, my ships have all miscarried, my creditors 430
grow cruel, my estate is very low, my bond to the Jew is for-
feited, and, since, in paying it, it is impossible I should live,
all debts between you and I are cleared, if I might but see you
at my death. However, let it be as you wish, if your love won't
persuade you to come, let not my letter. 435

PORTIA

O love! Finish your business and be gone.

BASSANIO

Since I have your consent to go away,
I will be quick. Until I come again
No bed will dare be guilty of my stay, 440
Nor our reunion rest ever detain.

They exit

Enter Shylock, Salanio, Antonio, and the Jailor

SHYLOCK

Jailor, watch him, don't talk to me of mercy,

This is the fool that lends out money free.

Jailor, watch him.

ANTONIO

Hear me out, good Shylock.   445

SHYLOCK

I'll have my bond, do not speak against my bond.

I have sworn an oath that I will have my bond.

You called me "dog" before you had a cause,

But since I am a "dog," beware my fangs.

The Duke shall grant me justice. I wonder,   450

You worthless jailor, that you are so lax,

To bring him out here at his request.

ANTONIO

Please, just hear me speak.

SHYLOCK

I'll have my bond, I will not hear you speak.

I'll have my bond, so therefore speak no more.   455

I'll not be made a soft and dull eyed fool,

To shake my head, relent, and sigh, and yield

To Christian intercessors: don't follow me,

I'll have no "speaking," I will have my bond.

Exit Shylock

SALANIO

This is the most impenetrable dog   460

That ever lived with men.

ANTONIO

Leave him alone.

I'll follow him no more with pointless prayers:

He seeks my life, his reason I know well.
I have delivered many from his debt,   465
Many who moaned about his usury.
And so he hates me.

SALANIO

I am sure the Duke
Will not permit this compensation to be collected.

ANTONIO

The Duke cannot deny the course of law: 470
All contracts foreigners sign with us in Venice
Will be in jeopardy if it's denied;
And much impugn the justice of the State.
The trade and profit of this city depend
On other nations. Therefore go.   475
These griefs and losses have diminished me,
Tomorrow I won't have a pound of flesh
To give to my most bloody creditor.
Well, Jailor, on! Pray God Bassanio comes
To see me pay his debt, then I don't care.   480

They exit

Enter Portia, Nerissa, Lorenzo, Jessica, and a man of Portia's

LORENZO

Madam, although I say this to your face,
You have a noble and a true idea
Of god-like friendship, witnessing what strength
You urged and bear the absence of your lord.
But if you knew the man you show this honor,   485
How true the gentleman to whom you send relief,
How dearly he loves my lord, your husband,
I know you'd be the prouder for your work
Than normal rules of courtesy afford.

PORTIA

I never did repent for doing good — 490
Nor will I now. For with companions
Who oft converse and spend much time together,
(Whose souls do equally bear the yoke of love),
There naturally must be a similarity
Of physical attributes, of manners and of spirit; 495
Which makes me think that this Antonio,
Being a bosom friend of my lord Bassanio,
Must also resemble my lord. If that is true,
How low the cost and what a paltry price
To purchase the very semblance of my soul 500
From out of the state of hellish cruelty.
This comes too close to praising my own self,
And so, no more. Let's talk of other things:
Lorenzo, I commit into your hands
All management and running my estate, 505
Until my lord's return. For my own part,
I have sworn a secret vow to heav'n,
To live in prayer and contemplation,
Only attended by Nerissa here,
Until her husband and my lord return. 510
There is a monastery two miles off,
And there we will reside. I truly ask you
Not to refuse these obligations,
Which my love and some necessity
Now lays upon you. 515

LORENZO

Madam, with all my heart,
I will obey you in all fair commands.

PORTIA

My servants do already know my mind,

They will acknowledge you and Jessica
In place of lord Bassanio and myself.   520
Take good care, until we meet again.

LORENZO

Good thoughts and happy hours be with your trip.

JESSICA

I wish your ladyship her heart's content.

PORTIA

I thank you for your wish. I am well pleased
To wish it back to you, take care, Jessica.   525

Exit Jessica and Lorenzo

Now Balthazar, as ever I've found you honest and true,
Let me find you truer, take this letter,
With all the strength a man can muster, go,
Full speed to Padua and see you put it
In my cousin's hands, Doctor Bellario.   530
And take whatever notes and garments he gives,
And bring them back with unimaginable speed
Straight to the transport docks, the common ferry,
Which sails to Venice. Waste no time with words,
And now be gone, or I'll be there before you.   535

BALTHAZAR

Madam, I go with all appropriate speed.

PORTIA

Come Nerissa, I have plans at work
That you don't know of yet. We'll see our husbands
Before they think of us.

NERISSA

Will they see us?   540

PORTIA

They will Nerissa, but in such disguises,
That they will think we're well endowed

With what we lack. I'll bet you any odds
When we are both dressed up like two young men,
I'll prove the prettier rascal of the two, 545
And wear my dagger with a braver flair,
And speak with reedy voice caught right upon
The cusp of boy changing to man, and turn
My dainty step to manly stride; and brag
Of brawls like heated youth, and tell quaint lies 550
How honorable ladies sought my love,
Which when I denied they fell sick and died,
And I could do nothing. Then I'll repent,
And wish that after all I had not killed them.
And twenty of these puny lies I'll tell, 555
And men shall swear I'm just finished school
About twelve months ago. I have in my mind
A thousand vulgar tricks of these cocky lads,
Which I will practice.

NERISSA

Why, we'll turn tricks with men? 560

PORTIA

My, what a question?
As if you were a crude commentator.
But come, I'll tell you my whole scheme
When we are in my coach, which waits for us
At the park gate; so let us fly away, 565
For we must cover twenty miles today.

They exit

Enter Lancelot and Jessica

LANCELOT

Yes truly; you must watch out, the sins of the father are laid
upon the children, so I'm telling you: I truly fear for you. I
was always straight with you, so now I'll speak my agitation

70

in this matter. But be merry, for truly, I think you are damned. 570
There is but one hope that can do you any good, and that is
but a kind of "bastard" hope.

JESSICA

And what hope is that pray tell?

LANCELOT

By the Holy Mother, you can hope that your father begot you
not, so you're not the Jew's daughter. 575

JESSICA

That really is a "bastard" hope. To hope to be a bastard, so the
sins of my mother can be laid upon me.

LANCELOT

Truly then, I fear you are damned by both father and mother;
for when I shun Scylla (your father), I fall into Charybdis
(your mother); so you're sunk both ways. 580

JESSICA

I will be saved by my husband; he has made me a Christian.

LANCELOT

Truly then, he's more to blame; there's already enough of us
Christians, as many as can live next to each other and be
good neighbors; this making more Christians will raise the
price of hogs; if we all become pork eaters, soon we won't 585
have a rasher of bacon on the coals for any price.

Enter Lorenzo

JESSICA

I'll tell my husband, Lancelot, what you say. Here he comes.

LORENZO

I will grow jealous of you quickly, Lancelot, if I find you cor-
nering my wife like this.

JESSICA

Nonsense, you need not fear us, Lorenzo. Lancelot and I 590
are at odds. He tells me plainly there is no mercy for me in

heaven because I am a Jew's daughter; and he says you're not a good member of the community, because in converting Jews to Christians, you raise the price of pork.

LORENZO

I'll answer to the community better than you do, knocking 595
up the negro's belly; isn't the Moor fat with your child, Mister
Lance-A-lot?

LANCELOT

So that's more reason: there's more of the Moor; but if she
be less honest than a woman, that's more than I took her for.

LORENZO

How every fool can play upon a word! I think the best form 600
of wit will soon be considered silence, and discourse become
appropriate only among parrots. Go, servant, bid them prepare for dinner.

LANCELOT

Isn't that already done, sir, since they all have stomachs?

LORENZO

Good grief, what a wit-splitter you are. Then tell them to 605
"prepare dinner."

LANCELOT

That is done, sir, but "lay" is the word.

LORENZO

Then will you get laid?

LANCELOT

Not so neither, sir, I know my duty.

LORENZO

Enough quibbling, or will you spill the whole wealth of your 610
wit in one spurt? Please understand a plain man in his plain
meaning: go to your cohorts, ask them to lay the table, serve
the meat, and we will come into dinner.

LANCELOT

As to the table, sir, it shall be served on, as to the meat, sir, it
will be covered. As to your coming into dinner, sir, why let it 615
be as your disposition and fancy *dic*-tate.

Exit Lancelot

LORENZO

Oh deft discernment, in every word a twist.
This fool has planted in his memory
An army of *bons mots*; but I do know
So many fools employed in higher place, 620
Tricked-out like him, who for a pesky pun
Obscure the matter. How are you, Jessica?
And now, good sweet, tell me your thoughts,
How do you like the lord Bassanio's wife?

JESSICA

Past all expression. It is most just 625
That lord Bassanio live a righteous life
Having such a blessing in his lady,
He finds the joys of heaven here on earth.
So if on earth he is not worthy now,
Then he should never come to heaven. 630
Why if two gods should play some heavenly match,
And lay a wager on two earthly women
And Portia be one: there must be something else
Added to the other, in this poor rude world
Portia has no equal. 635

LORENZO

And such a husband
You have with me, as she is for a wife.

JESSICA

Woah, best ask my opinion of that.

LORENZO

I will in time, first let us go to dinner.

JESSICA

No, let me praise you while I still have an appetite.   640

LORENZO

No, please wait, let it serve as table talk,
Then whatever you say will blend with other things
And I'll digest it.

JESSICA

Well, I'll serve you up.

They exit

ACT 4

Enter the Duke, the Magnificos, Antonio, Bassanio, and Gratiano

DUKE

What, is Antonio here?

ANTONIO

Ready, so please your grace.

DUKE

I am sorry for you that you are come to answer

A stony adversary, an inhumane wretch,

Incapable of pity, void, and empty   5

Of a single drop of mercy.

ANTONIO

I have heard

Your grace has taken great pains to moderate

His rigorous course; but since he stands obdurate

And there's no lawful means to shield me now   10

From his envy's reach, I do oppose

My patience to his fury and am armed

To suffer with tranquility of spirit

The utmost tyranny of his great rage.

DUKE

Now go and call the Jew into the court.   15

SALARINO

He is ready at the door, he comes my lord.

Enter Shylock

DUKE

Make room, so he can stand before our face.

Shylock, the world thinks, and I do too,

That you're prolonging pretense of your malice

75

To this act's last hour, and then it's thought   20
You will show your mercy and compassion to be
More remarkable than your present cruelty.
And where now you still exact the penalty,
Which is a pound of the Merchant's flesh,
You will not only stop this punishment,   25
But, touched with human gentleness and love,
Forgive a portion of the principal,
And cast an eye of pity on his losses
That have of late so crowded on his back,
Enough to weigh a royal merchant down,   30
And prompt compassion for his troubled state
From stony bosoms and rough hearts of flint,
From stubborn Turks and Tartars never trained
In acts of kindness nor of courtesy,
We all expect a gentle answer, Jew.   35

SHYLOCK

I have informed your grace of my intent,
And by our holy Sabbath I have sworn
To have what's due for the forfeit of my bond.
If you deny it, let the danger light
Upon your charter, and your city's freedom.   40
You'll ask me why I'd rather chose to have
A weight of carrion flesh, than to receive
Three thousand ducats? I'll not answer that:
But say it humors me. Is it answered?
What if my house were troubled with a rat,   45
And I were pleased to give ten thousand ducats
To have it poisoned? Does that answer you?
Some men detest a pig roasted with mouth agape,
Some men go mad if they behold a cat,
And others, if they hear the bagpipe whine,   50

Cannot contain their urine for the emotion.
Passion's master sways it to the mood
Of what it likes or loathes; now for your answer:
As there is no firm reason to be given:
Why he cannot abide a gaping pig? 55
Why he a harmless, familiar pussy cat?
Why he a woolen bagpipe, and surrendr'ng
Must yield to such inevitable shame
As to offend himself being offended.
So I can give no reason, nor will I not, 60
More than a lodged hate, and a certain loathing
I bear for Antonio, which makes me follow
A losing suit against him. Are you answered?

BASSANIO

This is no answer, you unfeeling man,
To excuse the geyser of your cruelty. 65

SHYLOCK

I am not bound to please you with my answer.

BASSANIO

Do all men kill the things they do not love?

SHYLOCK

Hates any man the thing he will not kill?

BASSANIO

Every offense is not a "hate" at first.

SHYLOCK

What you'd have a serpent sting you twice? 70

ANTONIO

If you think you can reason with the Jew,
You might as well go stand at ocean's edge
And tell the tide to stop before it's full,
Or try to ask a question of the wolf:
Why does the ewe bleat for her little lamb? 75

You may as well forbid the mountain pines
From wagging their high tops and make no noise
When they are fretted by the gusts of heaven.
You may as well do anything most hard,
As seek to soften that — what harder than 80
His Jewish heart. Therefore I implore you
Make no more offers, use no further means,
But with all brevity and diligence
Let me have judgement, and the Jew his will.

BASSANIO

For your three thousand ducats here is six. 85

SHYLOCK

If every ducat in six thousand ducats
Were in six parts and every part a ducat
I would not take them. I will have my bond!

DUKE

How will you hope for mercy, if you give none?

SHYLOCK

I do no wrong, what judgement shall I dread? 90
You have among you many purchased slaves,
Which like your asses, and your dogs and mules,
You use in abject and in slavish ways,
Because you bought them. Shall I say to you:
Let them be free, marry them to your heirs? 95
Why sweat under your burdens? Let their beds
Be made as soft as yours, and let their palates
Be nourished with such sav'ries: you will answer
The slaves are ours. So I do answer you.
The pound of flesh which I demand of him 100
Is dearly bought, it's mine, and I will have it.
If you deny me, your Law is a joke,
There is no force in the decrees of Venice.

I stand for judgement, answer, shall I have it?

DUKE

Upon my power I will dismiss this court,   105
Unless Bellario, a learned Doctor,
Whom I have sent for to determine the case,
Comes here today.

SALARINO

My lord, outside there waits
A messenger, new come from Padua,   110
With letters from the Doctor.

DUKE

Bring us the letters, call the messenger.

BASSANIO

Cheer up, Antonio. Keep your courage yet!
The Jew will have my flesh, blood, bones, and all
Before you lose one drop of blood for me.   115

ANTONIO

I am the sickly, neutered ram of the flock,
Designated for death, the weakest fruit
Falls fastest to the ground, so let me drop.
Bassanio you cannot be better employed
Than to stay alive and write my epitaph.   120

Enter Nerissa as Clerk

DUKE

You come from Padua, from Bellario?

NERISSA

From both. My Lord Bellario greets your grace.

BASSANIO

Why do you whet your knife so earnestly?

SHYLOCK

To cut what is due from that bankrupt debtor.

GRATIANO

Then hone your knife not on your shoe's sole, 125
But on your soul, harsh Jew. No metal,
No, not even the hangman's ax is half as sharp,
As your sharp hatred. Can no prayers pierce you?

SHYLOCK

No, none that you have wit enough to make.

GRATIANO

O be damned, you execrable dog, 130
If you're alive then justice stands accused.
You almost make me waver in my faith,
And take Pythagoras' opinion
That souls of animals infuse themselves
Into the bodies of men. Your feral spirit 135
Governed a wolf who hung for human slaughter.
Even from the gallows his scruffy soul floated
Into the womb of your unholy Mum,
Infused itself in you. For your desires
Are wolvish, bloody, starved, and ravenous. 140

SHYLOCK

'Til you can talk the seal off from my bond,
You only offend your lungs to speak so loud:
Repair your wit, good youth, or it will fall
To endless ruin. I stand here for law.

DUKE

This letter from Bellario recommends 145
A young and learned Doctor to our court.
Where is he?

NERISSA

He's right here, waiting next door
To know your answer, whether you'll admit him.

DUKE

With all my heart. Some three or four of you   150
Go give him courteous welcome to this place.
Meanwhile the court will hear Bellario's letter.

*Your Grace, please understand at the receipt of your letter
I am very sick, but the instant that your messenger came
a young Doctor of Rome was with me in loving visitation,* 155
*his name is Balthazar. I acquainted him with the case in
controversy, between the Jew and Antonio the Merchant.
We poured over many books together; he is furnished with
my opinion, which is improved with his own learning, the
greatness whereof I cannot commend enough. At my urging* 160
*he brings my opinion with him to fulfil your Grace's request
in my place. I entreat you, let his lack of years be no imped-
iment to prevent him your most reverend estimation. For I
never knew so young a body with so old a head. I leave him
for your Grace to accept into the court; this trial will better* 165
publish his praise.

Enter Portia for Balthazar

DUKE

You hear what the most learned Bellario writes,
And here (I take it) is the Doctor come.
Your hand. Have you come from old Bellario?

PORTIA

I did my lord.   170

DUKE

You are welcome; take your place.
Are you acquainted with the difference
That holds this present question in the court?

PORTIA

I am informed thoroughly of the case.
Which is the Merchant here, and which the Jew?   175

81

DUKE

Antonio, old Shylock, please come forward.

PORTIA

Is your name Shylock?

SHYLOCK

Shylock is my name.

PORTIA

The suit you pursue is strange in nature,
Yet the prescribed rules governing Venetian Law   180
Cannot find fault with you as you proceed.
You stand within his power, do you not?

ANTONIO

Yes, so he says.

PORTIA

Do you confess the bond?

ANTONIO

I do.   185

PORTIA

Then the Jew must be merciful.

SHYLOCK

On what compulsion must I? Tell me that.

PORTIA

The quality of mercy is not forced,
It falls like gentle rain from heaven
On the earth below. It is twice blessed: 190
It blesses one who gives, and one who takes,
It's mightiest in the mighty, and becomes
The throned monarch better than a crown.
A scepter shows the force of temporal power,
With attributes of awe and majesty,   195
Being the source of dread and fear of kings,
But mercy is above this sceptered sway,

It is enthroned within the hearts of queens,
It is an attribute of god herself,
And earthly power shows itself to be godly 200
When mercy tempers justice. Therefore Jew,
Though your plea is with justice, consider this,
That in the course of justice, none of us
Will see salvation. We must pray for mercy,
And that same prayer, can teach us all to do 205
Most merciful acts. I have spoken all this
To mitigate the justice of your case,
Which if you follow, the strict court of Venice
Must perforce rule against the Merchant there.

SHYLOCK

My deeds are on my head. I crave the Law, 210
The penalty and forfeit of my bond.

PORTIA

Is he not able to pay off the loan?

BASSANIO

Yes, here I provide it for him in the court,
Here's twice the sum, if that will not suffice,
I will be bound to pay it ten times over: 215
And forgo my hands, my head, my heart.
If this does not suffice, it does appear
That malice trumps the truth. I beg you
Rein in the Law to your authority:
Do the right thing (and a little wrong), 220
And curb this cruel devil of his will.

PORTIA

It must not be, there is no power in Venice
Can alter an established decree.
It would be recorded as a precedent
And many an error by the same example 225

Will overwhelm the State. It cannot be.

SHYLOCK

A Daniel come to judgement, yes, a Daniel.

O wise young Judge, how I do honor you.

PORTIA

Please, may I see the bond in question?

SHYLOCK

Here it is, most reverend Doctor, here it is.   230

PORTIA

Shylock, three times the value he offers you.

SHYLOCK

An oath, an oath, I have an oath in heaven.

Shall I lay perjury on my soul?

No, not for Venice.

PORTIA

The bond's term is up,   235

And lawfully by this the Jew may claim

A pound of flesh, to be cut off by him

Nearest the Merchant's heart; be merciful

Take three times the money, let me tear up the bond.

SHYLOCK

When it is paid according to the tenure.   240

It does appear you are a worthy judge

You know the Law, your exposition

Has been most sound. I charge you by the Law,

Whereof you are a well deserving pillar,

Proceed to judgement. By my soul I swear,   245

There is not power in the tongue of man

To alter me. I stay here for my bond.

ANTONIO

I implore the court immediately

To give the judgement.

PORTIA

    Why then here it is: 250

    You must prepare your bosom for his knife.

SHYLOCK

    O noble Judge. O excellent young man.

PORTIA

    For the intent and purpose of the Law

    Does fully authorize the penalty,

    Which here appears due upon the bond.   255

SHYLOCK

    It's very true. O wise and upright Judge,

    You are much older than your looks betray.

PORTIA

    Therefore lay bare your bosom.

SHYLOCK

    Yes, his breast.

    So says the bond, does it not noble Judge?   260

    Nearest his heart, those are the very words.

PORTIA

    It is so. Is there a scale prepared to weigh the flesh?

SHYLOCK

    I have it ready.

PORTIA

    Shylock, is there a surgeon standing by

    To stop his wounds so he won't bleed to death?   265

SHYLOCK

    It is not specified in the bond?

PORTIA

    It is not so expressed, but what of that?

    It's good you do this much for charity.

SHYLOCK

    I find nothing here, it's not in the bond.

PORTIA

Come Merchant, have you anything to say?   270

ANTONIO

But little: I am armed and well prepared.

Give me your hand, Bassanio, take good care.

Grieve not that I am fallen to this for you,

For here my fortune shows herself more kind

Than is her custom. It is her habit   275

To let a wretched man out live his wealth,

To view with hollow eye and wrinkled brow

An age of poverty. From the ling'ring penance

Of this misery she now cuts me off.

Commend me to your honorable wife,   280

Tell her the process of Antonio's end,

Say how I loved you, speak well of me in death.

And when the tale is told, let her be the judge

Whether Bassanio had not once a Love.

Don't repent that you will lose a friend,   285

And he won't repent that he pays your debt.

For if the Jew will cut but deep enough,

I'll pay it instantly, with all my heart.

BASSANIO

Antonio, I am married to a wife,

Which is dear to me as life itself,   290

But life itself, my wife, and all the world,

Are not esteemed by me above your life.

I would lose all; I sacrifice them all

Here to this devil, to deliver you.

PORTIA

Your wife would give you little thanks for that   295

If she were near to hear you make the offer.

86

GRATIANO

I have a wife whom I protest I love,

I would she were in heaven, so she could

Entreat some power to change this dog-like Jew.

NERISSA

It's good you make the offer behind her back,   300

Your sacrifice could end domestic peace.

SHYLOCK

And these be Christian husbands! I have a daughter,

I wish she'd married Barabbas or one

Of his descent, rather than a Christian.

We trifle time, proceed now to the sentence.   305

PORTIA

A pound of that same Merchant's flesh is yours,

The court awards it, and the Law does give it.

SHYLOCK

Most rightful Judge.

PORTIA

And you must cut this flesh off his breast,

The Law allows it, and the court awards it.   310

SHYLOCK

Most learned Judge, a sentence, come prepare.

PORTIA

Wait a minute, there is something else.

This bond here gives you not a jot of blood.

The words expressly state a pound of flesh.

Then take your bond, take your pound of flesh,   315

But in the cutting of it, if you but shed

One drop of Christian blood, the State of Venice

Will confiscate your land and property,

by the Laws of Venice.

GRATIANO

O upright Judge, 320
Note, Jew — O learned Judge.

SHYLOCK

Is that the Law?

PORTIA

See for yourself — you can read the act;
Since you demand justice, be assured
You will have justice more than you desire. 325

GRATIANO

O learned, Judge, note Jew, a learned Judge.

SHYLOCK

I'll take this offer then, pay three times the bond,
And let the Christian go.

BASSANIO

Here is the money.

PORTIA

Wait, the Jew will have real justice, wait, no rush, 330
He will have nothing but the penalty.

GRATIANO

O Jew, an upright Judge, a learned Judge.

PORTIA

Therefore prepare to cut off the flesh
And shed no blood, and cut nor less nor more,
Than just a pound of flesh. If you take more 335
Or less than a just pound, be it so much
As makes it lighter or heavier in total weight
By the twentieth part of the smallest division,
Of one poor scruple, that is, if the scale tips
Even a hair's breadth in the weighing, 340
You die, and all your goods are confiscated.

GRATIANO

A second Daniel, a Daniel, Jew,

Now infidel, I have got you cornered.

PORTIA

Why does the Jew pause? Take your penalty.

SHYLOCK

Give me my principal and let me go.   345

BASSANIO

I have it ready for you, here it is.

PORTIA

He has refused it openly in court.

He will have only justice and his bond.

GRATIANO

A Daniel, I repeat, a second Daniel,

I thank you Jew for teaching me that word.   350

SHYLOCK

Shall I not even have my principal?

PORTIA

You will have nothing but the penalty,

To be taken here at your peril, Jew.

SHYLOCK

Why then the devil give him good from it;

I'll stay no more to argue.   355

PORTIA

Not so fast, Jew.

The Law has yet another hold on you.

It is enacted in the Laws of Venice,

If it be proven against an Alien

That by direct, or indirect attempt   360

He seek the life of any Citizen,

The party against which he has conspired

Will seize one half of his goods, the other half

Comes to the coffers of the State treasury;
And the offender's life lies at the mercy   365
Of the Duke, solely, and beyond appeal.
In this predicament, I'd say, you stand,
For it appears by evident proceedings,
That indirectly, and directly too,
You have conspired against the very life   370
Of the defendant: so you have incurred
The legal penalty I've just described.
Kneel down then, and beg the Duke for mercy.

GRATIANO

And beg us for permission to hang yourself.
Since all your wealth belongs now to the State,   375
The value of a rope's beyond your means,
So you'll be hanged now at the State's expense.

DUKE

So you shall see the difference in our spirits,
I pardon you your life before you ask:
For half your wealth goes to Antonio,   380
The other half comes to the general State,
Which courtesy may settle as a fine.

PORTIA

Yes, for the State, not for Antonio.

SHYLOCK

No, take my life and all, pardon not that.
You take my house, when you take the funds   385
That do sustain my house; you take my life
When you do take the means by which I live.

PORTIA

What mercy can you show him, Antonio?

GRATIANO

A free noose, nothing else for God's sake.

ANTONIO

    If it pleases my lord the Duke and all the court,   390
    to drop the fine for one half of his goods;
    I'm satisfied, if he will let me have
    The other half in trust to transfer it
    Upon his death to the gentleman
    Who recently stole his daughter.   395
    And two provisions more: that for this favor
    He forthwith become a Christian;
    The second: he in court record a gift
    Of all he does possess at point of death
    Unto his son Lorenzo and his daughter.   400

DUKE

    He will do this, or else I will take back
    The pardon I have pronounced here.

PORTIA

    Are you satisfied Jew? What do you say?

SHYLOCK

    I am satisfied.

PORTIA

    Clerk, draw up a deed of gift.   405

SHYLOCK

    I pray you give me leave to go from here.
    I am not well, send the deed after me,
    And I will sign it.

DUKE

    Then be gone, but do it.

GRATIANO

    In Christ'ning you will have two godfathers —   410
    Had I been the judge, you should have had ten more,
    To send you to the gallows, not the font.

                Exit Shylock

DUKE

Sir, I invite you to come home to dinner.

PORTIA

I humbly beg your Grace's pardon,

But I must leave tonight for Padua.   415

And so I must immediately set forth.

DUKE

I am sorry, sir, your time is not your own.

Antonio, reward this gentleman,

For in my mind you are bound to him.

Exit Duke and his train

BASSANIO

Most worthy gentleman, my friend and I   420

Have been acquitted by your wisdom here

Of griev'ous penalties, in thanks thereof

Three thousand ducats due to pay the Jew

We give to you to compensate your pains.

ANTONIO

And stand indebted over and above   425

In love and service to you ever more.

PORTIA

He is well paid who is well satisfied,

And I, by freeing you, am satisfied.

So in that I account myself well paid.

My mind has never turned more mercenary.   430

Please recognize me when we meet again.

I wish you well, and so I take my leave.

BASSANIO

Dear sir, I must most fervently insist

You take some remembrance from us as a tribute

Not as a fee. Please grant me two requests: 435

Not to deny me, and to pardon me.

PORTIA

You press me hard, and therefore I will yield,
Give me your gloves, I'll wear them for your sake,
And for your love, I'll take this ring from you.
Do not withdraw your hand, I'll take no more.   440
And you for love will not deny me this?

BASSANIO

This ring, good sir, alas, it is a trifle,
I will not shame myself to give you this.

PORTIA

I will have nothing else, but only this,
And now, I think, my mind is fixed on it.   445

BASSANIO

There's more depends upon this ring than worth.
I'll buy for you the dearest ring in Venice,
And find the highest price by public auction,
But please excuse me this one, just one time.

PORTIA

I see sir you are gen'rous with your talk.   450
You taught me first to beg and now it seems
You teach me how a beggar should be answered.

BASSANIO

Good sir, this ring was given me by my wife,
And when she put it on she made me vow
That I should neither sell, nor give, nor lose it.   455

PORTIA

That excuse serves many a wealthy man,
And if your wife is not a mad woman,
And knows how well I have deserved this ring,
She won't remain your enemy for life
For giving it to me. Well, peace be with you.   460

Exits

ANTONIO

My lord Bassanio, let him have the ring,
Let his deserving and my love
Be valued 'gainst your wife's commandment.

BASSANIO

Go Gratiano, run and overtake him.
Give him the ring and bring him, if you can,   465
To Antonio's house. Away, be quick.

Exit Gratiano

Come you and I will go now straight away,
And in the early morning we will both
Fly towards Belmont, come Antonio.

They exit
Enter Portia and Nerissa

PORTIA

Inquire where lives the Jew. Give him this deed,   470
And let him sign it. We'll away tonight,
And be home a day before our husbands.
This deed will be most welcome to Lorenzo.

Enter Gratiano

GRATIANO

Fair sir, I'm glad I caught up with you —
My lord Bassanio upon more advice,   475
Has sent you here this ring, and does request
Your company at dinner.

PORTIA

That cannot be.
His ring I do accept most thankfully,
So do please tell him that, and furthermore,   480
I ask you: show my youth old Shylock's house.

GRATIANO

That I will do.

NERISSA

Sir, I would speak with you.

I'll see if I can get my husband's ring

Which I did make him swear to keep forever.   485

PORTIA

I bet you can; we'll have the standard oath,

That they did give their rings away to men.

But we'll defy them, and out-oath them too.

Away, be quick, you know where I will wait.

NERISSA

Come good sir, will you show me to his house?   490

They exit

ACT 5

Enter Lorenzo and Jessica

LORENZO

    The moon shines bright. On such a night as this,

    When the sweet wind did gently kiss the trees

    And they did make no noise, on such a night

    Troilus, I think, mounted the Trojan walls,

    And sighed his soul out toward Greek army tents,   5

    Where Cressida lay that night.

JESSICA

    On such a night

    Did Thisbe, fearful, trip over dewdrops,

    And see the Lion's shadow before the beast,

    And run away dismayed.   10

LORENZO

    On such a night

    Dido stood with willow branch in hand

    Upon the wild sea banks, and called her Love

    To come again to Carthage.

JESSICA

    On such a night   15

    Medea gathered the enchanted herbs

    That did renew old Jason.

LORENZO

    On such a night

    Did Jessica steal from the wealthy Jew,

    And with a profligate Love run from Venice   20

    As far as Belmont.

JESSICA

On such a night
Did young Lorenzo swear he loved her well,
Stealing her soul with many vows of faith,
Not one that is true.   25

LORENZO

On such a night
Did pretty Jessica (like a little shrew)
Slander her Love, and he forgave her.

JESSICA

I would "out night" you if no one had come.
Listen. I hear footsteps of a man.   30

Enter Messenger

LORENZO

Who comes so fast in silence of the night?

MESSENGER

A friend.

LORENZO

A friend, what friend? Your name, if you are friend.

MESSENGER

Stephano is my name, and I bring word
My mistress will be here at Belmont   35
Before the break of day. She wanders hours
By holy crosses where she kneels and prays
For happy wedding days.

LORENZO

Who comes with her?

MESSENGER

None but a holy hermit and her maid.   40
Tell me, is my master yet returned?

LORENZO

He is not, nor have we heard a word from him.

But let's go in, come sweet Jessica,
Let us ceremoniously prepare
Some welcome for the mistress of the house.   45

Enter Lancelot the Clown

LANCELOT

Woo hoo! Woo hoo! Oh hoo woo — hoo woo!

LORENZO

Who calls?

LANCELOT

Woo who. Did you see Master Lorenzo and Mistress Lorenza,
who woo?

LORENZO

Stop woo-hooing, man, I'm here.

LANCELOT

Who's where? Where's who?   50

LORENZO

Here!

LANCELOT

Tell him there's a courier come from my master with a horn-
ucopia of good news. My master will be here by morning.

Exit

LORENZO

Sweet soul, let's go and wait for them within,
And yet why bother, why should we go inside?   55
My friend, Stephano, please announce
To all within the house your mistress is at hand,
And bring your musicians out into the air.
How sweet the moonlight sleeps upon the bank,
Here we can sit and let the sound of music   60
Creep into our ears. The soft stillness of night
Invites the touch of strings' sweet harmonies.
Sit Jessica, look how the floor of heaven

Is thickly inlaid with patterns of bright gold.
There's not the smallest orb you can perceive,   65
But in its movement like an angel sings
A chorus for the young-eyed Cherubim.
Such harmony resides in immortal souls,
But while this muddy cloak of gross decay
Entraps us close within, we cannot hear it.   70
Come ho, awake Diana with a hymn,
With tender plucking pierce your mistress' ear,
And with sweet music draw her home.

JESSICA

I am never merry when I hear sweet music.

Music plays

LORENZO

Because your spirit's focused and awake.   75
When you observe a wild and wanton herd,
A stampede of youthful and unbroken colts,
Bucking and kicking, bellowing and neighing loud,
Which is the natural condition of their blood,
If they do hear by chance a trumpet sound,   80
Or any notes of music touch their ears,
You will observe them stand together still,
Their savage eyes turned to a modest gaze
By the sweet power of music. Therefore Ovid
Wrote that Orpheus charmed trees, stones, and floods,   85
Since nothing is so hard and full of rage
That music for a time can't transform its nature.
A man that has no music in himself
And is not moved by sweet harmonies,
Is fit for treason, plotting, and spoils;   90
The motion of his spirit dull as night,
And his affections dark as Hades' pit.

Let no such man be trusted: listen to the music.

Enter Portia and Nerissa

PORTIA

That light we see is burning in my hall.

How far that little candle throws its beams, 95

So shines a good deed in a wicked world.

NERISSA

When the moon shone we did not see the candle.

PORTIA

So greater glory dims a lesser light,

A substitute shines brightly as a king,

Until the king arrives, and then his state 100

Empties itself like an inland brook

Into the flood of ocean: music, listen!

Music

NERISSA

It's your musicians, madam, from the house.

PORTIA

Nothing is good unless we can compare it:

I think this sounds much sweeter than by day. 105

NERISSA

Silence gives it that virtue, madam.

PORTIA

The crow sings just as sweetly as the lark

With no one there to listen. And I think

The nightingale, if she sang by day,

When every goose is cackling, would be thought 110

No better a musician than the wren.

How many things, praised to true perfection,

Are seasoned by the season in which viewed?

Peace! How the moon sleeps with her lover, Endymion

And would not be awaked. 115

Music ends

LORENZO

That's Portia's voice,

Unless I'm much deceived.

PORTIA

He knows me like the blind man knows the

Cuckoo: by my terrible voice.

LORENZO

Dear lady, welcome home!   120

PORTIA

We've been off praying for our husbands' health.

We hope they've prospered for our holy words,

Are they returned?

LORENZO

Madam, they're not back yet.

A messenger has come before you now   125

To announce their arrival.

PORTIA

Go in, Nerissa,

Give orders to my servants that they make

No mention of our absence from the house,

Nor you Lorenzo, Jessica, nor you.   130

A trumpet sounds

LORENZO

Your husband is nearby, I hear his trumpet.

Fear not, we are no tattle-tales.

PORTIA

This night, I think, is only daylight sick.

It grows a little paler, and it's day,

A cloudy day when the bright sun is hid.   135

Enter Bassanio, Antonio, Gratiano, and their followers

BASSANIO

We could trade day for darkest night,

If you would walk in place of the bright sun.
PORTIA

Let me be your light, but not taken lightly,
For a light wife will make a heavy husband,
And never Bassanio heavy 'cause of me.   140
God sort it out; you're welcome home, my lord.
BASSANIO

I thank you, madam, please welcome my friend.
This is the man, this is Antonio,
To whom I am so infinitely bound.
PORTIA

In all senses you should be bound to him,   145
For as I hear, he was much bound for you.
ANTONIO

No more than I am well acquitted of.
PORTIA

Sir, you are very welcome to our house.
It needs appear in other ways than words,
So I'll spare us all the usual polite speech.   150
GRATIANO

By the moon up there, I swear you do me wrong —
In truth, I gave it to the judge's clerk,
Would his nuts be shorn that I had done so.
Who knew, love, you would take it so to heart?
PORTIA

A quarrel, what already? What's the matter?   155
GRATIANO

About a hoop of gold, a paltry ring
That she did give me, whose inscription reads
Like a knife cutter's hackneyed verse
On a blade: "Love me and leave me not."

NERISSA

Why talk about the poem or its worth?   160
You swore to me when I gave it to you,
That you would wear it 'til your hour of death,
And it should lie with you deep in your grave.
So, if not for me, then for your vehement oaths,
You should have had respect and kept the ring.   165
Gave it to the judge's clerk? Ha, I know well
That clerk will never have a hair on her face.

GRATIANO

He will, if he lives to be a man.

NERISSA

Yes, if a woman lives to be a man.

GRATIANO

Now by this hand I gave it to a youth,   170
Like a boy, a little runt of a boy,
No taller than yourself, the judge's clerk,
A chatterbox that begged it as a fee,
I could not say no for all my heart.

PORTIA

You were at fault, I must be plain with you,   175
To part so easily with your wife's first gift,
A ring glued on your finger with an oath,
And so welded with faith into your flesh?
I gave my love a ring and made him swear
Never to part with it, and here he stands.   180
I dare swear for him he would not part with it,
Or pluck it from his finger for all the wealth
That the world offers. Now, in truth Gratiano,
You give your wife a cruel cause for grief,
If it were me, I too would be irate.   185

BASSANIO

    Well then I better cut my left hand off,

    And swear I lost the ring defending it.

GRATIANO

    My lord Bassanio gave his ring away.

    Right to the judge that begged him for it.

    Deserved it too. And then the boy, his clerk,   190

    Who took great pains in scribing, he begged mine.

    Both man and master wouldn't take a thing

    But those two rings.

PORTIA

    What — the ring I gave you my lord?

    Not that, I hope, which you received from me.   195

BASSANIO

    If I could add a lie atop this fault,

    I would deny it; but you see my finger

    Doesn't have the ring upon it, it is gone.

PORTIA

    Then equally void is your false heart of truth.

    By heaven, I will not come into your bed   200

    Until I see the ring.

NERISSA

    Nor I in yours, 'til I see mine again.

BASSANIO

    Sweet Portia,

    If you did know to whom I gave the ring,

    If you did know for whom I gave the ring,   205

    And could conceive for what I gave the ring,

    And how unwillingly I parted with the ring,

    When nothing could be given but the ring,

    You would soften the strength of your displeasure.

PORTIA

If you understood the virtue of the ring,   210
Or the worthiness of she who gave you the ring,
Or your own honor in preserving the ring,
You would not have parted with the ring.
What man is so completely unreasonable,
That if you'd chosen to defend the ring   215
With any zeal, he'd lack the modesty
To keep a thing that holds such ceremony?
Nerissa teaches me what to believe:
On my own life, I'll bet a woman has the ring.

BASSANIO

No, by my honor madam, by my soul,   220
No woman has it, but a jurist, a Doctor,
Who refused three thousand ducats from me,
And begged me for the ring, which I denied him,
And suffered him to go away displeased,
Even he that preserved the life   225
Of my dear friend. What should I say, sweet lady?
I was enforced to send it to him after.
I was beset with shame and courtesy,
My honor would not be tarnished by
Such ingratitude. Pardon me good lady.   230
And by these blessed candles of the night,
Had you been there, I think you would have begged
Me then to give the ring right to the worthy Doctor.

PORTIA

Don't let that Doctor dare come near my house,   235
Since he has got the jewel that I once loved,
The one which you did swear to keep for me.
I will become as liberal as you,
I'll not deny him anything I have:

No, not my body, nor my husband's bed.   240
Know him I will, I am well sure of it.
Don't leave home, watch me with a thousand eyes
Like Argos, if you don't, if I'm left alone,
By my honor, which is still my own,
I'll have the Doctor for my bedfellow.   245

NERISSA

And I his clerk; so be forewarned,
You leave me now to be my own protection.

GRATIANO

Well, best you do, let me not take him then,
For if I do I'll scar the young clerk's pen.

ANTONIO

I am th'unhappy subject of these quarrels.   250

PORTIA

Sir, please, grieve not,
You're welcome here despite it all.

BASSANIO

Portia, forgive me this unwilling wrong,
And in the hearing of these many friends
I swear to you, even by your own fair eyes   255
Where I can see myself.

PORTIA

Do you hear that?
In both my eyes he doubly sees himself,
One in each, to swear by your double cross-eyed self,
Yes, there's an oath of merit.   260

BASSANIO

No, but hear me.
Pardon this fault, and by my soul I swear
I never more will break an oath with you.

ANTONIO

Once I did lend my body for his wealth,
And without him that has your husband's ring 265
It would have been my death. I dare be bound again:
My soul upon the forfeit, that your lord
Will never more break faith with you in deed.

PORTIA

Then you will be his guarantor: give him this,
And bid him to keep it better than the other. 270

ANTONIO

Here, lord Bassanio, swear to keep this ring.

BASSANIO

By heaven, it is the same one I gave the Doctor.

PORTIA

I got it from him. Pardon Bassanio,
For with this ring the Doctor lay with me.

NERISSA

And pardon me, my gentle Gratiano 275
For that same runt of a boy, the Doctor's clerk,
With this ring, did lie with me last night.

GRATIANO

Why this is like mending highways
In summer before the potholes have formed.
What are we cuckolds before we even deserve it? 280

PORTIA

Don't speak so rudely, you'll all be amazed.
Here is a letter, read it at your leisure.
It comes from Padua from Bellario,
There you will find that Portia was the Doctor,
Nerissa was her clerk. Lorenzo here 285
Will witness I set forth as soon as you,
And only now returned; I have not yet

Entered my house. Antonio you are welcome,
And I have better news in store for you
Than you expect. Unseal this letter now,   290
And you will find three of your cargo ships
Have suddenly come home most richly fit.
You'll never know by what strange accident
I chanced upon this letter.

ANTONIO

I'm dumbstruck.   295

BASSANIO

Were you the Doctor, and I knew you not?

GRATIANO

Were you the clerk who means to make me cuckold?

NERISSA

Yes, but a clerk who never means to do it,
Unless he lives to be a man.

BASSANIO

Sweet Doctor, you will be my bedfellow,   300
When I am absent, please lie with my wife.

ANTONIO

Sweet lady, you have given me life and living,
For here I read for certain that my ships
Are safely come to port.

PORTIA

And you Lorenzo?   305
My clerk has some good news to comfort you.

NERISSA

Yes, and I'll give it to him without a fee.
Here I do give to you and Jessica
From the rich Jew, a special deed of gift
Of all his property upon his death.   310

LORENZO

Fair ladies you drop manna in the mouths
Of starved people.

PORTIA

It is almost morning.
And yet I am sure you've not had your fill
Of hearing fully of these events. Let's go in,   315
And hold your fierce interrogations there,
And we will answer all things faithfully.

GRATIANO

Let it be so. The first hard question is:
(And my Nerissa must swear to answer it)
Whether she'd rather wait until tonight,   320
Or go to bed right now two hours 'til light.
But when the day does come, I'll wish it dark,
Until I'm lying with the Doctor's clerk.
Well, while I live, I'll fear no other thing,
So sore, as keeping safe Nerissa's ring.   325

They exit

END